The Learning Commons

The Learning Commons

Seven Simple Steps to Transform Your Library

Pamela Colburn Harland

 LIBRARIES UNLIMITED

AN IMPRINT OF ABC-CLIO, LLC
Santa Barbara, California • Denver, Colorado • Oxford, England

Library of Congress Cataloging-in-Publication Data

Harland, Pamela Colburn.
   The Learning Commons : Seven Simple Steps to Transform Your Library / Pamela Colburn Harland.
      p. cm.
   Summary: "This simple guide provides valuable insights for transforming an out-of-date public, school, or academic library into a thriving, user-centric learning commons"— Provided by publisher.
   Includes bibliographical references and index.
   ISBN 978–1–59884–517–4 (pbk. : acid-free paper) — ISBN 978–1–59884–518–1 (ebook)
1. School libraries—United States. 2. Information commons—United States. 3. Libraries and students—United States. 4. Public services (Libraries)—United States. 5. High school libraries—United States—Case studies.
Z675.S3H38   2011
027.8—dc22   2010046019

ISBN: 978–1–59884–517–4
EISBN: 978–1–59884–518–1

15 14 13 12 11   1 2 3 4 5

This book is also available on the World Wide Web as an eBook.
Visit www.abc-clio.com for details.

Libraries Unlimited
An Imprint of ABC-CLIO, LLC

ABC-CLIO, LLC
130 Cremona Drive, P.O. Box 1911
Santa Barbara, California 93116-1911

This book is printed on acid-free paper ∞

Manufactured in the United States of America

To John Skelton, for being my inspiration to write a book, read the classics, watch the birds, and live without regrets.

Contents

Illustrations

Acknowledgments

Thank you to JoAnn Guilmett from the Plymouth State University Lamson Library and Learning Commons for helping me to create the initial presentation on which this book is based. Thank you to Elaine Allard for teaching the librarians of New Hampshire about the ideas behind a learning commons.

Thank you to Russ Harland, who read and reread the manuscript during one cold and stormy February vacation. You are the best editor, thesaurus, fire builder, snow blower, and husband a girl could ask for. I'm the lucky one, and I couldn't have done this without you!

Thank you to Casey Brough for always making me laugh, helping to make my vision a reality, and for being the best library Web site designer anywhere (frealz). He'll be finishing his MLS in 2011 and looking for a library of his own. I'm just saying.

Thank you also to Mark Halloran for the support he has given to the library, and to Dr. Ethel Gaides for the support she has given to the librarians.

Thank you to Bruce Parsons, Maura Dougherty, Aaron Blais, Lena MacLean, Bob Schrier, Kathy Boyle, the PRHS book club, and the amazing faculty and administration at Plymouth Regional High School.

Thank you to Erika Frank for sharing a well-designed vision in librarianship, and to Heather Armitage for inspiring me to keep writing.

Thank you to Susan Ballard, Kristin Whitworth, Sara Zoë Patterson, Dot Grazier, Sharon Silva, Kathy Lane, and the other librarians from NHSLMA. You all make me proud to be a librarian in New Hampshire!

Thank you and big love especially to Cheryl Downing, Janice Whitaker, Everett Colburn, Martha Borsh, and John Skelton.

Introduction

Our libraries are no longer book rooms, and adding computers into the mix does not make them computer rooms. We need flexible spaces with well-selected resources, adaptable furniture, current technology, collaborative services, and a well-trained staff in one space where we can guide our students to be smart researchers and learners prepared for the future. We need to create a space that fosters collaborative work and social interaction amongst all of our users.

Whether you call it a learning commons, an information commons, a research commons, a media center, or a library does not matter. At my high school, we continue to refer to our space as a library when talking to students, staff, administration, parents, and the general public. When talking to librarians, we explain that we originally based our library program on the learning commons model at Plymouth State University's Lamson Library. Our common goal is that we provide a single centralized location for all users to get help on all of the complex issues of teaching, researching, and being a student or teacher at our school. We offer a central and collaborative hub for instruction, research, and learning, as well as a place to use innovative technologies and information resources.

The learning commons idea is the library world's answer to the changing informational and technological needs of today's learners as well as a shift in pedagogical models. In addition to providing traditional library services, a learning commons model integrates technological and instructional elements typically found in other departments outside of the library (technology help desks, guidance departments, tutoring services, writing centers, etc.). A proper learning commons is also constantly reevaluating the program and looking toward new ways to provide a space in which all users are learning collaboratively, experimenting with technologies, and customizing the space. In our learning commons, we encourage our faculty to serve as facilitators, and our students to have open discussions free of evaluation.

One of the most common misconceptions that I have found when describing the learning commons idea to the uninitiated is that people often assume that I am recommending that we simply invest money into more computers or other technologies into the current library. People mistakenly believe that broadening services in the area of technology and spending a lot of money will magically shift a library into a learning commons, but I'm here to tell you differently. In order to truly transform your library, you do not need to spend a lot of money on computers, digital cameras, scanners, and e-books. All you need to do is to shift your way of thinking from being the protector of information and resources to being the advocate for unfettered access to information and resources. Much like the way in which we share information through open-source software and tools, a learning commons is a space staffed by professionals who want to make all resources and information sources available to all users.

We recently had several faculty members retire, and as we prepared for the transition and the parties, I went through our archived yearbook collection to find some classic snapshots of our retirees. The frightening thing to me was looking at the pictures of our classrooms and instructional facilities from 30 years ago and noticing that not much had changed. The hairstyles back then were funny, and everyone wore glasses. Other than that, the students are sitting at desks in rows, listening to teachers lecture, taking notes with their textbooks beside them. The chalkboards have been replaced with interactive whiteboards but are being used for the same thing. Teachers now simply type their lecture notes into PowerPoint instead of writing in chalk. Information is available at your fingertips today, so how has your educational environment changed to incorporate this immediate access to the world of information? The world has changed so drastically in the last 10, 20, and 30 years, but has your school and library integrated those changes into your daily practice?

Questions to Ask Yourself

- Does your school need a library when most information can be accessed in the classroom using the Internet?
- What is it that your library offers to your users in addition to accessing information?
- Are you doing it well?
- Could you do it better?
- How can you increase and improve services?
- Could you make a *shift* in your service?

Today, our students now have access to a virtual high school, and schools all over the country are looking toward moving more coursework online so that users have continual access to the information and resources that an old-fashioned brick-and-mortar school and classroom provides. As your building moves toward additional online learning environments, what will happen to your current library? With access to so much information and the exponential growth of new technologies, learners and teachers of today need a professional to guide them. We need to be sure that we are providing the right kind of space, resources, and services for all of our users.

A Note to Administrators

The ideas described in this book are inexpensive, sometimes cost-saving ideas. They will not necessarily revolutionize your organization, but they will transform your library users into passionate researchers, social learners, and responsible and well-prepared members of the twenty-first century. These seven simple steps will streamline your library users' information seeking and processing methods, provide your library users with the ability to adapt easily to the future, and encourage all of your faculty and staff to work together.

Our main goal is to set up a single help desk where users (students, patrons, faculty, staff, and administration) can request assistance for anything. The highly skilled and well-trained library employees cover the help desk and have the capability, resources, and access to information to answer almost any question that a user may ask (from typical library questions, to technology questions, to school resources and supplies, and much more). Users have a more satisfying experience because they don't have to guess where to go for what question, the library staff is utilized for a variety of information-type requests (we provide better service, with the same amount of personnel), and several different school operations are now streamlined—saving you and your employees time and money.

In order to adapt easily to changing roles and technologies, our spaces and staff need to remain flexible. Changes should be made based on what the user's needs are, not on what is more convenient for the library staff. Barriers of all types need to be removed and exchanged for a trust in all of our users. Technology needs to be ubiquitous, and most of it should be transparent to users.

The most difficult aspect of this shift in library experience is helping a librarian to change from being a guardian and protector of information and resources to being a guide to information and resources.

A librarian also needs to develop the skills in technology planning and use. A computer is no longer just a computer. In addition to being a word-processing machine and Internet-browsing device, a computer can be a communication tool (video phone, conferencing device, instant messenger, etc.) with a built in webcam and microphone. A computer can be a social equalizer, providing students who do not have access to the Internet at home the means to create a social identity online to rival those of the most upper-class students. A computer can be a digital portfolio of all of a user's academic work and digital personal life. Computers may be mobile, they may have installed digital media readers, and they may have movie-editing software. Every library needs a professional who can understand what the users need and provide timely access to those resources. But most importantly, a librarian needs to be an advocate for all learners.

Finally, all of these changes need to be documented and shared with you, the stakeholders, and the entire community. People enjoy seeing quantifiable statistics with any change, and library services are easy to count and keep track of. Expect publications in the form of monthly statistical reports as well as newsletter-type stories with descriptions of the changes and the impact on the library and the rest of the community.

In order for this transformation to be successful, the entire school community needs to be open to sharing resources between departments, creative in utilizing budgetary line items, and open to genuine collaboration between professionals.

1

Step One: User-Centered

A successful library is user-centered, not technology-centered. Every decision needs to emphasize making our spaces, services, resources, and tools more valuable to all of our users. User-Centered Design is a popular software design philosophy and process in which the user's needs are given priority over all other options. By taking this philosophy and transferring it to library redesign, we can make our libraries the most user-friendly spaces on campus.

Before your next physical or virtual library redesign, think about the following questions.

Questions to Ask Yourself

- Who are the users of your library? Students, teachers, administrators, parents, community members, staff? Try to think of everybody who might use your library in the future.
- What is your users' purpose? Research, collaboration, content creation, lesson planning and creation, reading, silent study, utilizing the various tools, socializing?
- What do they need to access while in the library? Computers, wireless Internet, office supplies, photocopier, printers, scanners, books, USB drives, CDs, TV/DVD players, textbooks, classmates, instructors, current news, novels?
- Do your users have prior experience with a library? What was that experience like?
- What information can you provide to make their experience easier? Signs, labels on the book stacks, handouts?
- How do your users *expect* the library to work? They may expect a library to be quiet, complicated, confusing, dusty, etc.
- Does your documentation answer the question you intended it to answer? Once you hand out the guide to using online databases, do students raise their hands and ask for clarification? Do students know where to find the proper documentation?
- What are your users looking for when they walk through the door or connect to your site? A new book to read, a place to work together with classmates, help on citing sources, a pen to use during their next class?
- Is there an obvious place to ask questions? Do your users want to approach this place? Do your users intuitively approach your desk or the checkout desk? Where do you want your users to go for most questions?

It may be difficult for you to focus on what a student is thinking when they walk into your library without being influenced by what you learned in school about what a library should look like—or more likely, what your own library experience may be. Many libraries use a legacy-centered model, using the same design ideas that librarians have used for decades and even centuries. Your library may have an ingrained tradition that you hesitate to change because it has worked for years. The first step to shifting your library is to let go of some of these guidelines. The shift is brought about by the need for new services, tools, and resources. As you consider making the shift, be sure to focus on what your users need and not on the services, tools, spaces, and resources themselves.

One basic change that you can make is in the use of language in your library. Most libraries are categorized, arranged, and labeled using language from the lexicon of librarians. But do your *users* know what these terms mean? Circulation, reference, periodicals, OPAC, ILL, bibliographies, and other terms can be confusing to new users. Instead, use simple and descriptive terms that any user can understand. Instead of "circulation," use "checkout desk." Instead of "reference," use "information desk." Instead of "periodicals," use "magazines." Instead of "ILL," use "borrowing from another library." Talk to your users. What do they call the book return? The book-drop? The drop-box? Label the areas of your library clearly and then use that language while talking to your users.

One of our goals is to teach students about the structure of libraries, but let's make sure that they know how to use our resources before we begin teaching them the specialized language of our profession. We do not want to send students off to the next academic level without an understanding of these terms, so be sure to include lessons on specialized language with more advanced classes.

Another aspect of user-centered design is taking all of the cultural information that you have and combining it with the observations you have made, the interviews you have conducted, and all other collected data to analyze and brainstorm your results. When you talk to students, they may not be able to articulate the exact ideas that you implement. Instead, they will point you in the right direction. You may observe a student who seems annoyed at having to come back to your desk to get a second red marker because the one she was using had dried up. Note this reaction and consider some different alternatives. You may overhear a student saying to a teacher, "I wish it was easier to know which database to go to." Take that information and move towards a Web site remodel (such as that displayed in Figure 1.1) and handout redesign. Think about how you might explain what each database is best used for in future collaborative lessons. Users will not be able to tell you specifically how to redesign your Web site, but their questions and frustrations will guide you in the right direction. When you hear complaining and whining, prick up your ears and think about why your users are complaining and

Figure 1.1.   How Are Students Using Your Resources?

whining. If you can make a change to prevent future complaints, do it right away. Keep a keen eye on how your users utilize your facility and the resources held within. The more we understand how our users are using our resources and adapt our facilities toward them, the more relevant our libraries will become. As you learn more about your users, you will see that their needs are constantly changing, and the best learning commons will be able to adapt to their users' needs.

The Plymouth Model

In 2006, we had a basic legacy-design library. We had computers, a traditional client/server online public access catalog, and a seldom used, sparsely populated, and static Web site. On our shelves, we had 11,000 items with an average year of publication of 1987 with extremely low circulation for over 900 students. Our print reference collection was 14 percent of our collection with an average age of 1992 while our fiction collection was 8 percent with an average of 1983. Yearbooks, gluesticks, and other resources that students wanted to use on a daily basis were kept behind the large counter that served as the information desk. This desk essentially spanned across the entire front half of the library. The counter served as a large barrier between the library staff and the users. It also protected our most-used resources from the users who needed them.

We provided faculty with a huge selection of audiovisual equipment, borrowing, troubleshooting, and taping services. We had a room filled with dust-collecting slide projectors, never-used laser-disc players, and a historical archive of projector bulbs going back nearly 40 years. We had televisions and VCRs hooked up to our cable connection allowing the professional librarian to record television broadcasts for classroom use.

We also had a large selection of seldom-used print periodicals. The magazines were housed in spinning literature racks that blocked out the cover of each magazine, only revealing the top two inches of each cover page, occasionally revealing the actual title of the magazine. All of our newspapers were located on three-foot-long bamboo poles preventing the current issues from getting stolen, but when it came down to it, nobody ever actually read the newspapers, let alone tried to steal them.

We had a security system that went off several times per day as students found it entertaining to place a library book in an unsuspecting student's backpack. The library staff would get flustered, the students would all laugh, and we would inevitably find a book about human sexuality or something equally humiliating for the backpack wearer.

Incoming freshmen would come in for an introductory lesson on how to use the library. Each class came in with their English teachers, and the librarians would show them a digital slide presentation with the rules of the library. We talked about checkout limits (five items for two weeks), using our online catalog even though the students lacked computer access during the presentation, and the rules of our library (especially what students were not allowed to do, such as no food, no headphones, and no games of any kind). Students were excited to enter the library but were soon distracted and bored while watching the presentation and listening to us talk about what they were not allowed to do in the library.

Nothing seemed crazy or out of the ordinary. It was business as usual for most libraries for the past several decades. It was standard operating procedure for a lot of public high school libraries in New Hampshire at the time. When looking critically at our 2006 legacy-model, we were hard-pressed to find significant value in our system. We decided that we needed to shift our current methods, systems, resources, and services to add some value to everything that we did.

We spent that school year watching our users and how they used our library. We talked to students about what they really needed in a library. We listened to teachers who came in requesting resources and then watched to see how they used them. Finally, we created a detailed survey and sent it out to all students, faculty, administration, staff, and parents.

Sample Survey Questions from the PRHS Student Survey

What do you use the PRHS Library for? (Check all that apply)
- □ Find books for assignments
- □ Use computers
- □ Find books for pleasure reading
- □ Do homework or study
- □ Group work
- □ To get help from the librarians
- □ Use library resources (laminator, office supplies, copy machine, etc.)
- □ Meet with friends to socialize
- □ Meet with tutor
- □ Work on digital portfolio
- □ Other

Please rate the following resources and services:

	Very valuable to me	Valuable to me	Somewhat valuable to me	Not valuable to me	I don't know / Never used
Pleasure reading books					
Books for research					
NoodleBib/MLA formatting information					
Print Magazines and Newspapers					
AudioBooks					
Photocopy machine					
Laminator					
Cameras, jump drives, voice recorders					
Color printer					
Scanners					
Library staff					
Digital Portfolio information and resources					
Tutors					

Do you read more because of information or resources that you've found at the PRHS Library?

- □ Yes
- □ Uncertain
- □ No

Are you able to do better research because of the information (books and databases) and/or resources (librarians, supplies, computers) that you've found at the PRHS Library?

- □ Yes
- □ Uncertain
- □ No

Are you able to complete projects more easily because of the information (books and databases) and/or resources (librarians, supplies, computers) that you've found at the PRHS Library?

- □ Yes
- □ Uncertain
- □ No

Based on our questions, you can see we had already begun using several new initiatives: online citation generators, digital portfolio information, audiobooks, and digital cameras. We created different surveys for school employees and for parents, too. (See Appendix A for more sample surveys.) We spent the summer of 2007 reviewing the survey results and making some very basic changes to our library.

We purchased some inexpensive office supply organization bins. We recommend that you not use old coffee cans, shoe boxes, and milk crates. We strive to establish and maintain a professional atmosphere in our learning commons. We are trying to expose our users to what a professional experience will be like when they are not in school. Creating a professional atmosphere also raises expectations and helps to set a tone for being in the library and using the library's resources.

We created a workshop-type area near the checkout desk where students could help themselves to markers, glue sticks, scissors, paperclips, staplers, rulers, colored pencils, and note cards (Figure 1.2). Make this area a self-help supply center. Allow students open access to these supplies—you'll be surprised at how many of the supplies do *not* disappear. You will have an initial onslaught of disappearing scissors and rulers, but as the students get used to the fact that these supplies are not going away, your users will become more trustworthy and honest about returning the supplies. Refrain from believing that these supplies are "your" supplies and that anything removed from the area and not returned is a personal assault on you or the library.

A secondary benefit of providing users with unlimited office supplies is that teachers will notice that their classroom supplies are remaining stocked. Students tend to use the supplies provided in a centralized location like the library. Your principal will notice that teacher supply accounts are not being fully spent, so you may approach him or her with a request to increase the library supply account. Encourage your principal to talk to teachers about their supply accounts, and you may end up with a budget increase. We currently have about 750 students at our school and we spend

Figure 1.2.   The Workshop

approximately $1,500 per year on office supplies. This includes the supplies that we need to run the library, too.

Another benefit to keeping your supplies in organizational bins is portability. Students can take an entire bin of markers or colored pencils to their table to work, rather than bringing their work up to the supplies. Some user-centered libraries put together a bin for each table containing a glue stick, a pair of scissors, a ruler, markers, paper clips, and Post-It notes. Watch your users and see how they are using supplies to create finished products. Put yourself in the shoes of a student and ask how you would want supplies to appear.

Think about creating a workshop-type environment for your users. In order to create a comfortable atmosphere, go out and look at professional copy centers with work spaces. What is so inviting about a professional copy center? Look at furniture, counter space, resource allocation, placement of materials, signage, computers, and staff. Be open minded and watch how the users are using and enjoying the space. Pick out the aspects that you could realistically implement in your library. Perhaps the furniture is unreasonable because the cost would prohibit you from purchasing new soft seating, low tables, and bookshelves with outfacing book covers. Be mindful about changes that you could make in your space, and your users will appreciate it.

Another easy tip for creating a user-centered library is creating a school textbook reserve (see Figure 1.3). We asked all departments to give us a copy of all current textbooks. We recorded the textbook numbers in a spreadsheet, tattle-taped the textbooks, and put a small checkmark in pencil on the inside front cover (to have an easy way to check whether the books belonged to us or to a student). We put all of the textbooks on

Figure 1.3.   Textbooks in the Library

a bookshelf and simply labeled them "for library use only." Your textbook shelves will be in regular disarray because they will be constantly in use. Students will request fewer trips to their lockers and have fewer excuses for not completing their homework.

Our students come to the high school from eight different K–8 schools. Three of those schools have wonderful libraries with full-time librarians providing instruction, collection development, and reader guidance. Two of those schools have combined school-public libraries with the expectation that the students will use only the children's section and leave the adult books to the public. The other three schools have very small "book rooms" with access to a part-time aide. Obviously, our incoming student users have a huge range of prior experience. We try to even the playing field early by inviting the eighth-graders from the schools with the smallest library facilities to visit our library in the spring before they start at the high school. We have the students follow a scavenger hunt through the library and work with the guidance department to include a school tour.

We also encourage all of our freshman English and social studies teachers to bring their students to the library as early in the school year as possible in order to expose all of our freshmen to the resources available to them in our library. For their first visit, we have the class sit down in a quiet section of our library. We talk about the resources to which they now have access in their high school library. We pass around digital voice records, digital cameras, USB jump drives, iPods, audiobooks, and electronic book readers as well as books that we know they will like (see Figure 1.4).

Be sure to include several very short book talks about award-winning titles, new nonfiction filled with colored pictures, and of course, every book talk should include a book about zombies and/or vampires. We then hustle them over to the computers and teach them how to log on to our school network and access our library Web site. If the classes are doing any kind of research project, we show them a single database and demonstrate to them how to use it for their specific assignment. Finally, we encourage the students to browse the periodicals, book stacks, and library displays on their own. My favorite part of these visits is hearing the questions that the students have about the library—ranging from practical ("How many books can we check out?") to wary ("Will an alarm go off if I bring back an overdue book?"). Changing from a text-heavy slide presentation about what they cannot do in the library to hands-on entertaining and integrated lessons keeps our freshmen engaged and allows them to make more relevant connections to the library resources.

Figure 1.4. Technology Accessories

"No phones, no food, no hats" signs are not necessary in any room, especially in our learning commons. They are negative and constant reminders that set the tone of your space as prohibitive. If you must post rules, be creative instead of restrictive. The rules at our library (see Figure 1.5) are posted by the sign-in books. Users appreciate the humor and understand the tone of the space as they first enter the room.

Figure 1.5. Rules of the Library

We noticed that we were subscribing to a number of expensive professional journals that were rarely being accessed. We decided that instead of attaching a routing list to the journals, we would photocopy the cover page and table of contents and send these packets of information to faculty members who might be interested in the contents. We suddenly had lines of faculty waiting to get their hands on the newest issues of the *English Journal* and the *Science Teacher*. With one student volunteer, you can increase usage of your professional journals by having the student make the photocopies, deliver the copies to the appropriate teacher mailbox, and handle any requests that you get for copies of articles or access to past issues. By publicizing available resources for our teachers, we increased use of these journals dramatically—many teachers were unaware that we had these titles available at all.

We heavily weeded our print reference collection based on access to electronic resources with the same information. We also moved a lot of our single-volume monograph titles from reference to the regular circulating collection. Items that are alphabetical multivolume sets are difficult to circulate, but sets that are divided by topics are also generally moved to our circulating collection. In addition to weeding reference, we heavily weeded the circulating collection. We gave away hundreds of titles. This quickly updated our collection as library users suddenly believed that we had added a lot of new titles without our actually having added any. Weeding is a crucial step to transforming any out-of-date library. Preserving inaccurate and out-of-date materials on your library shelves is one way to demonstrate to your users just how irrelevant print materials really are.

We discarded most of the unused audiovisual equipment from our back room and weeded through the light bulbs, taping supplies, and other outdated resources. This freed up space for spreading out our professional collections, digital audiovisual equipment, and video collections. Now when teachers walk into our back room, they barely recognize it as the same space. It is much neater and less crowded. Keeping library space neat and organized is crucial to demonstrating a professional atmosphere for your users.

We also ordered some very simple wall-mounted magazine display racks, such as those in Figure 1.6. We looked for racks that had Plexiglas fronts so that users could see the entire front cover of each periodical title. We placed our newspapers in an easy-to-use newspaper display rack (Figure 1.7), much like the racks that we saw at the large chain bookstores. We used to dust the periodical racks weekly because users never touched them. We now have to check the displays daily to reorganize, re-alphabetize, and straighten out this popular section.

Virtual Library Redesign

We redesigned our library Web site based on what our users needed and wanted. In the middle of our observational and evaluative year, our users found an immediate need that we chose to implement quickly. When we wanted to make changes to the library Web page, we submitted our requested changes to the school's webmaster who would edit our Web site using Dreamweaver (a Web design and development tool). Often, coded text I would send would not translate between vanilla HTML and Dreamweaver, and almost every change required explanation and often more than one revision. Most changes were done within the week, but total overhauls were scheduled for the summer—and it was

Figure 1.6.   Magazines

only September 2006 when I was faced with this new Web-driven shift in culture. We found that students were asking for links to commonly visited Web sites over and over again. Things like: "What was that CIA site that you told our class about this morning?" or "What is the best crossword puzzle generator Web site?" I wanted to be able to send the link right to the student's computer, and students expected that I could make this happen. We were looking for a tool that was free, quick, and easy to use; required no special software or tools; provided flexibility; and had no advertising. We wanted a tool that allowed us to focus on the content rather than the technology.

We initially chose to create the Web site as a wiki; however, a blog or other Web 2.0–based tool would have suited us just fine, too. We began sharing resources by adding links as students requested them and then began to set up a new page for each new research project (Figure 1.8). On each page, we provided links to Web sites and research hints that we wanted to share with the students. Since we also integrated e-books and virtual resources with our print volumes and brick-and-mortar space, we included access to them on our wiki page. Faculty loved it. Students loved it. We loved it!

Once you set up your own wiki page, you may realize that your teachers also want to share Web sites with their students—so give your wiki password to all faculty. Only

Figure 1.7. Newspapers

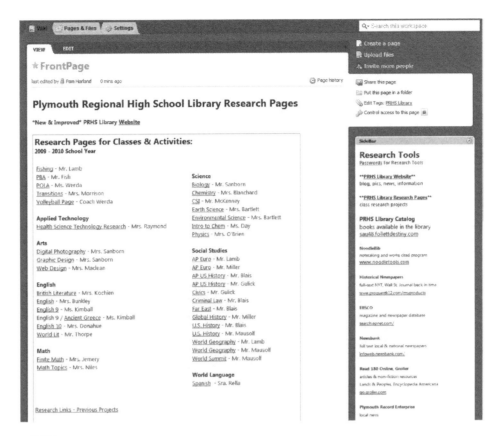

Figure 1.8. Wiki

two or three faculty members will actually use it to share Web sites at first, but any teacher who is assigning research will be directing their students to your wiki pages. Maybe *you* can see where this is going, but back in September 2006, I never would have believed it. By December 2006, we had the first students who wanted to share Web sites with their class-mates. Soon, you'll be giving out the password to entire classes at one time. We have nearly 800 high school students with full editing capability on 50-plus research wiki pages—and in four years, we have not had a single case of virtual vandalism.

As of 2010, and following these basic changes from a legacy designed library to a user-centered learning commons, we observed several statistical changes in our collection:

	2005–2006	2009–2010
Collection Size	11,000	17,000
Average Age of Collection	1987	1997
Student Population	900	750
Print Reference Collection	14% of total	5% of total
Average Age of Reference	1992	1992
Print Fiction Collection	8% of total	27% of total
Average Age of Fiction	1983	2005
Total Annual Circulation	1,248	10,337

All of the changes that you make will increase services to your users; engage, empower, and educate your users; and make your job easier. By utilizing simple and user-centered designs, you encounter success by offering increased services to your users. And because these tools are simple, elegant, and powerful, they empower those users. As your users gain expertise, they learn to utilize more effectively these simple tools that you have provided them. It isn't always about spending more money on more resources—in this case, it's as simple as taking your existing tools and placing them in a convenient and obvious place so that our users can help themselves. When you put the tools and resources in logical places, your users will eventually and intuitively learn to be more autonomous users of all types of tools and resources. We give them experiential context—we demonstrate where to go for certain types of basic information and resources, and then they extrapolate and apply their new information location skills toward new and more complex information retrieval and use.

Your To-Do List

✓ Survey your users and your nonusers.

✓ Listen to your users.

✓ Watch everything that your users do and don't do.

✓ Talk to students and teachers about your Web site—ask for feedback.

✓ Observe students using your Web site.

✓ Ask departments for a copy of the current textbooks to be housed in the library.

✓ Brainstorm and analyze all of your findings.

✓ Photocopy new issues of professional journals for faculty.

✓ Make your job easier by empowering your users.

✓ ($) Purchase professional office supply organizational bins for your office supplies.

2

Step Two: Flexible

Make your physical and virtual spaces as well as your policies flexible, scalable, sustainable, and easily adaptable. The news is filled with items such as headmasters removing all books from a private school library, some libraries moving all of their books into storage, and some libraries replacing reference books with e-books, while still others are adding rows of computers in between the bookshelves. Most libraries are not built for change. In fact, they are usually built for long-lasting preservation and permanence. The trouble with this scenario is that while the ideas and philosophies of libraries, librarianship, and information resources are changing quickly, librarians are literally stuck with physical spaces that are unable to adapt. Libraries that were designed before the big shift in technology integration and student-learning styles are not likely to meet the needs of today's users.

In order to prepare for the coming changes, purchase mobile shelving and furniture whenever possible. Most shelving and library furniture is completely static due to its weight, size, and safety issues for your users. However, some library furniture is ideal when looking at mobility and flexibility. Several library furniture companies are now selling affordable mobile shelving and display racks. These pieces of furniture range in price from $300 to $2,000. Some have hidden wheels so they look like motionless shelves, so your users will not be tempted to rearrange your library while you are not looking. It also will not look like you have carts of books left all around your library. Furniture companies are now designing mobile furniture in several different styles to fit in with the look of your school and library.

The twenty-first-century learner is looking for a space that allows for social and interactive learning. When planning your library space, consider how your physical and virtual spaces promote learning rather than distract from it. Students are not looking for private and singular study carrels at which to work. Today's students need spaces where they can meet with other students and be seen by other library users, as seen in Figure 2.1.

In addition to purchasing furniture that is light and mobile, also be prepared to allow your users to move the furniture to suit their needs. This may be difficult to do, but give it a try. Allowing users to create and modify their own learning spaces should make it easier on you. By watching how users want to use the space and resources, you will get additional ideas for making your space even more user-centered. Allow the library design to be fluid, and the users will personalize their own learning environments. Some students will move a single chair to the book stacks in order to read in a quiet location surrounded by books. Other students will slide three tables together and get to work on a group project with the tables covered with

Figure 2.1.   Students Collaborating

books, laptops, markers, and poster board. Allow the users to experiment with what works best for them for each project that they do.

Also be sure to create library spaces that are scalable and sustainable. Your library configurations should make sense on days when you have a full house, as well as when you only have 10 or 20 users. Think about all of the different uses of the library space, and be sure that the space is comfortable for a wide variety of uses. Make sure that any redesign is sustainable. Building a library with dozens of empty shelves and a budget that will not fill them anytime soon is frustrating, rather than forward-thinking.

The Plymouth Model

With our new equipment budget, we were able to purchase one double-sided mobile shelving unit each year for the past three years. We made one of the units our new book display rack. We keep it full of new books, and when we have not ordered any new books in a long time, we create special themed displays on these racks. Another one of our mobile shelving units is used to display school textbooks. The final unit is used to display our reserve books. This has been extremely helpful in that we are able to leave the reserves in a consistent location, however; when a class comes into the library, we are able to wheel the books for that class up to their tables (Figure 2.2).

We placed several mobile shelving units in amongst our computer lab area and were surprised to observe how much serendipitous learning occurred every day. We noticed students, who had not gotten near the bookshelves in years, browsing through

Figure 2.2.   Mobile Shelving

the books that were now displayed on our mobile shelving. One student, who prided himself in not having opened a book since he arrived at our school, called me over to the mobile shelving one morning to show me that our new book on covered bridges in New Hampshire featured several structures that his family had built. We stood together and looked through the book until he decided that he would check it out and show it to his father at home that night. The next day, he returned the book and told me that he had never before seen his father read a book until he brought home the covered bridges book. A single moment of accidental learning, reading, and sharing like this was worth the cost of all the mobile shelving to me.

Along with most schools, we are faced with constant administrative mandates. Each year we have a new directive, such as digital portfolios, to which we need to adapt. The year in which digital portfolios were started in all New Hampshire public schools, our school hired a digital portfolio teacher who would design our school's portfolios, create rubrics, and assist the students in the creation of their digital portfolios. Our principal saw that students came to the library to ask for help and to utilize our technology, so he moved the digital portfolio teacher into the library. Directives like these require flexibility on all parts: furniture, attitudes, and technology. It seemed crucial to me that we set up a temporary space for our digital portfolios. The space looks permanent, but will not impact the library in any negative way if she either moves to her own classroom or we stop requiring our students to produce digital portfolios. We purchased a desk to match the other desks in the library, but did not build custom furniture. We did have a custom sign made to match the other signs in the library. While we want to create a consistent look in the library, we also simply want to be able to change it easily and inexpensively.

Virtual Flexibility

When creating your Web presence, be sure that it is flexible, sustainable, and scalable for your library. Migrate your Web presence to a wiki, blog, or some other easily updated tool. You need to be able to update your Web site instantly, and your users expect that you can do it. Some schools are using tools that enable teachers and librarians to create their own Web content, but if you are unable to make changes as the needs arise, suggest to your Web developer that your library page link directly to your own Web site. All librarians need to have constant and immediate access to a simple-to-use Web tool. Our presence on the Web needs to be flexible because the information that we provide is always changing based on the needs of our users. Content has to follow those changes and be dynamic. Your Web interface with your users may change all of the time based on what your users are looking for at different times. Blogs and other Web 2.0 tools are perfect because they are easy to edit, free, and simple to share. You can eliminate the webmaster by making updates to your Web site a one-step process.

Be sure to share the administrative passwords with the entire library squad and be sure that everyone is equally trained on simple updates. Nothing is more frustrating for your staff than if you control all Web content but are out of the library when an update or change is needed and they do not have access to the Web site. Sharing the responsibility also relieves you of some of the pressure.

Figure 2.3.   Web site on Mobile Device

Your Web site also needs to be sustainable. Do not set up a blog if you are unable to update it weekly. Once you set up a blog or wiki, practice making updates so that it becomes second nature for you. Updates do not have to be complex, but the more you make small changes, the easier it will become.

Also, if all you want to do is share your online databases with your users, create a simple Web page and link to it from the school's Web site, rather than creating a larger Web presence than you need. If your Web presence is scalable, you will have the ability to add single pages as the need arises. Do not create a complicated and deep Web site unless your users need that level of complexity for their information needs.

Finally, be sure to check your Web site on several different devices to see how it appears and how it operates due to differences in screen resolution, Web browsers, or the device presentation. We built our Web site at school, but when we went home and checked our site on higher-resolution monitors and lower-resolution laptops, we noticed some subtle differences. We also periodically check it on mobile phones (Figure 2.3) and any device that can browse the Web. We created this user-friendly Web site but if our users are unable to access the information from their device, then the site is useless in that instance.

Figure 2.4.   Web Site

Figure 2.5.   Embedded Widgets

The Plymouth Model Web Site

We began by using a free wiki for our users. After several years of simple updates, we decided to migrate to a more complex solution. We set up a customizable blog and content management system as our permanent Web site (http://prhslibrary.com). In our case, our wiki provider had drastically changed several features in the middle of the school year. We had been utilizing these features, and suddenly we had to retrain our 800 users with a new tool. We decided that because everyone relied on our Web site for such an incredible amount of information, we needed to set up a site that would not change based on a company's whim. We paid $30 for a customized URL and spent the last three weeks of the school year setting up our blog (Figure 2.4). We then had the summer to create several blog entries and to learn the intricacies of our new Web presence.

As the school year started, we had a lot of positive feedback. We received an e-mail from the state department of education asking if they could use our new Web site as a model for school libraries. Faculty members complimented us on the ease of locating all of the information that they needed on a single page. Students, who frequently balk at any change, were leaving positive comments on our blog entries.

On our new Web site, we provided the same information that we had on our wiki; but now it was better organized, we could better password-protect our database passwords page, and users could interact with the Web content. Our goal is to post a new blog entry each week. Sometimes we post book reviews, sometimes library or school events, and sometimes pictures of users in our library. We also integrated our picture-sharing site and our micro-blogging site as widgets embedded in our blog (Figure 2.5).

Be flexible in choosing new tools for your learning commons. Do not get stuck on brand names or specific models. Instead, be flexible enough to try out what your users demand. When deciding on a new technology device, pay special attention to simplicity and ease of use. Whatever you choose needs to be accessible to your least-savvy group of users.

Another component of flexibility is not abandoning your books when the next new device takes center stage on the news. However, you should take advantage of things such as e-readers as successful adjuncts to delivering print resources in the form that your users are asking for. If your users are all talking about Kindles and iPads, be open to trying out a new device that delivers information in an alternative way.

Policies

Make your library rules and policies more flexible. Look at rules such as limits on items checked out, loan length, and overdue blocks.

Questions to Ask Yourself

- Why do you currently have a limit on the number of items a user can check out?
- Why is your loan length the span that it is?
- Could your users benefit by a longer loan length?
- Can a user check out an item if they currently have overdue material?
- What would happen if you started allowing users to check out materials even if they had an overdue book?
- Is there a concern that all of your books would be checked out?
- Is it better that the books sit on a shelf unused?
- When is the last time you reevaluated your rules and policies?

We often find that our policies were established several years ago by an administration that was less flexible than it needed to be. If you base your policies on a legacy model, it is time to consider a new model. It is very easy and natural to continue with the inherited, existing rules from a prior administration. Policies to restrict users on the number of items to check out may make sense in a public library, where you do not have ready paths to resolution as you do in a school. At a school of any type, you know your users. You have access to your users daily. Do you also need to control the number of books that they check out? Of course, we do have rules and policies at our library, but we need to question them and think about what is best for our users. If your rules and policies are based on control rather than on what your users currently need, your library may benefit from a policy makeover.

There is also a vicious circle of checkout-limit policy. Libraries limit the number of books that a user can check out. That leads to users checking out a small number of books. That leads to low circulation statistics to share with your school board. That leads to a cut in book budget for the following year because the school board does not see that users are utilizing the print resources. That leads to fewer books available for librarians to provide to their users. And we are back at the beginning. Try to break the circle by making your policies more flexible—allow users to check out as many books as they want.

The Plymouth Model's Loan Policies

- Books, audio books, and electronic book-reading devices can be checked out for three weeks. These materials can be renewed unless another user has the item on hold.

- Digital cameras, video cameras, voice recorders, laptops, and USB jump drives can be checked out for one week. These materials can be renewed unless another user has the item on hold.
- Netbooks can be checked out overnight. They may be borrowed after school and are due the next day before classes begin.
- There is no limit to the number of library items a student can check out.
- The library also carries periodicals, newspapers, reference materials, videos, magazines, and textbooks, which are for in-library use only.

Personal Flexibility

Stay current with new technology and educational innovations. In addition to keeping our spaces flexible, we need to keep ourselves flexible, or we run the risk of making ourselves extinct in our own natural environments. We hear stories of schools cutting their librarians, and I have to wonder if these individuals are innovative and flexible leaders in their schools and in the field of librarianship.

Before a student comes into the library with a Web-enabled smartphone asking you to help get the project he created in Keynote Remote onto the library desktop, prepare yourself. Find out how smartphones work and how to sync one to a library desktop. The more we understand the world in which our students are growing up, the more relevant we become to their lives and, more importantly, to their learning.

To keep current with all of these new tools, set up a Google Reader (http://www.google.com/reader) or other aggregator account and subscribe to as many library and educational technology feeds that you can find. When you realize that you can't keep up with all of the entries, unsubscribe from the blogs that are either repeating what you already know (or have read elsewhere), overwhelming you with boring facts about the blog writer, or are too technical. Encourage the other librarians that you know and work with to set up Google Reader accounts—and now you can share blog entries with each other by simply clicking on the share button, instead of e-mailing the article to each other. By doing this, you are creating your own personal learning community.

If you live in an urban area or near a university, you may have access to lunchtime/brown-bag meetings and idea exchanges. Librarians and other individuals interested in information resources and educational technology will get together and discuss new ideas, share resources, and promote their current uses. If you don't have the luxury of a diverse group of professionals to meet with in person, you can do the exact same thing (minus the face-to-face interaction) via micro-blogging services. Set up a micro-blogging account, and you'll find a hundred librarians and other information resource professionals to follow. Read their updates daily and begin sharing your ideas. Soon, you will have followers and the ability to hold your own idea exchanges with your new professional learning network, from the convenience of your home or office, or even from a park bench via your Web-enabled smartphone.

When you share resources with your staff via old-fashioned e-mail, be sure to include where you obtained the information. Include a little note like "via the PRHS Library blog" with a link directly to the original statement. This shows your colleagues how valuable your professional learning network is and may lead them to establish their own.

Most of us are unable to predict the future, but we can stay current with mobile furniture, adaptable rules, and new innovations. Remaining flexible is the only way to function effectively in the complex and constantly evolving world of information and technology. Flexible libraries are easily reconfigured. We can also plan to be flexible in the face of whatever the future does hold for us.

Your To-Do List

✓ ($) Need new display furniture? Make it mobile!

✓ Create a library wiki or blog or other easily updated tool.

✓ Review your library rules and policies. Is there any leeway in making these rules more flexible?

✓ Setup an aggregator account in order to follow multiple blogs through one tool.

✓ Create a micro-blogging account and begin by following 100 librarians and technology educators.

✓ ($) Attend a conference every year.

✓ Make sure that all changes in your physical and virtual spaces are scalable and sustainable.

3

Step Three: Repetitive Questions

A major step in shifting your library is to change the way in which you deal with repetitive questions. This is a simple step that you can take in order to streamline services, which in turn will save time for you and your users. It is also a crucial time to teach students to be more autonomous. Self-reliant information seeking is a huge step in preparing our users for a future in which the information revolution continues to evolve.

Before you embark on streamlining services to all users, gather the entire library squad and agree on a common goal. If staff members are not clear on what type of information you are gathering, any kind of monitoring of questions will be useless. With every step in this guide, the first thing that the elite library squad must do is agree on the outcome. Be sure that each one of you share the goal of becoming a user-centered, collaborative, adaptive, and streamlined organization. Once everyone is in agreement, have your elite library squad keep track of questions that they answer more than once for an entire month. Monitoring your user's needs will help you to keep pace with the constantly evolving information environment.

The Plymouth Model

At Plymouth, we kept track of questions throughout the day with a simple clipboard system. We kept a clipboard with a notebook attached to it at the checkout desk. Every time we talked to a user, we added the discussion to the list on the clipboard. Sometimes we only had time to write down a couple of words, other times we would make a checkmark next to another question already on the list to indicate that we have answered the same question an additional time, and other times we wrote complete paragraphs explaining a detailed reference interview. We were surprised to see that after a week, we rarely added to the question list. We kept adding checkmarks to our list, but not many additional questions. After the second week, it became obvious how often we were repeating ourselves by answering the same questions over and over again.

Once the month was over, the entire library squad gathered together to review the list of questions. We also decided to brainstorm changes that we could make or information that we could share. We talked about improving signage, handouts, printed directions, locations of materials, and Web site design.

Figure 3.1.   Glue Sticks

Our most common question during the first year was, "Can I borrow a glue stick?" We were embarrassed when we saw how much time we spent handing glue sticks out to students (Figure 3.1). Four years later, we continue to refer to problems in our system as "glue sticks."

The answer to the "glue stick"–type questions were very simple. We created an office-supply workshop type area in the front of the library. Anywhere that students sit within the library, they can clearly see where all of the supplies and production tools are now located. We unlocked our supply cabinets, labeled the shelves and cabinets clearly, and opened up the area to all of our users (Figure 3.2). Librarians no longer are interrupted in the midst of a reference interview or a book talk in order to help a student find a glue stick. We are able to focus on our collection development, budgeting, and information resource lessons instead of glue stick–location instruction.

In addition to glue sticks, we provide our students with scissors, staplers, rulers, compasses, protractors, markers, colored pencils, Post-It notes, a three-hole punch, a paper cutter, pencils, a laminator, a photocopier, a printer, and a color printer. Keep track of what your users are repeatedly asking for at your library, and you will come up with your own user-centered list.

Some repetitive questions require a brief answer but complex directions. At the end of each book stack, we had call number–range labels. Several users, including teachers, would ask us how to locate a book even if they had the call number in their hands. Just because the call number–range labels seem clear to us does not mean that all of your users will be familiar with its use. We found two ways to handle this question depending on how users ask for help:

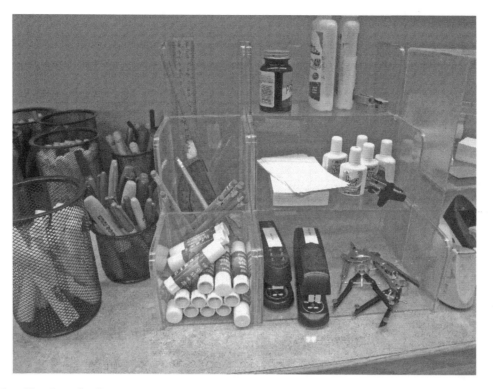

Figure 3.2.   The Supply Center

1. When a student has a specific call number for a specific book in hand, we walk them to the stacks and talk out loud about how to locate the books. For instance, we will say: "641.5 CHI? Oh yes, right over here. This shelf has all of the 640s and if I start on the top and scan down I see the 641.5s right here. Now let's look for CHI ... A, B, C ... here it is!" This type of instruction shows a new user how easy it is to find a book on the shelf without insulting them.
2. When a student is simply looking for the cookbooks, we quickly evaluate whether the student would like to be taken to the shelves or pointed to the shelves for their own browsing. Each instance is unique and often based on prior experience with that user.

In the second case, we found that if users wanted to be pointed to the shelves for their own independent browsing, they often still could not find the resources on the shelves from a brief description across the library. We decided to label all of our book stacks with aisle numbers in addition to the call number–range labels (Figure 3.3). Our users responded positively right away with the new aisle numbers. It became much easier to point a student to the books at the end of aisle four.

If you find yourself handing out glue sticks all day long, the glue sticks are obviously in the wrong place. However, we have found that in addition to the signs and the labels, and all of the information that we could provide, we still have students asking for a glue stick. We found that many times, students really just wanted to talk to us and the glue stick was a way for them to get the conversation started. We are all sensitive to the social needs of our students and are more than happy to engage with our students when that is what they really want from us.

Figure 3.3.   End of Stacks Label

Another frequently asked question was about in-text citations. We decided to create a series of handouts on formatting papers specifically for our students. We created one sheet on creating headers and formatting the top of a paper using the MLA format. We created another sheet on creating a Works Cited. As we developed these handouts, we wanted to keep them lighthearted but serious, so we decided to make the theme for our research "chocolate." Every citation that we wrote was based on a book, Web site, video, podcast, and lecture about chocolate. Students appreciate looking at what a final "Works Cited" should look like. Finally, we created our "in-text citation" sheet. We kept our examples very simple. We immediately had several English teachers hand out our in-text citation sheet to their students. Questions from students immediately lowered— and we continue to remain happy to help any student who still wants to talk to us about citing sources. (See Appendix B for sample handouts.)

We purchased a wall-mounted magazine rack to display our handouts (Figure 3.4). We labeled the rack clearly with simple signs at the top and easy-to-read labels for each handout. We then added a single copy to a binder that we keep at the checkout desk. When a library squad member notices that a handout is getting low, they can grab a copy from the binder and easily make photocopies. We noticed that this was faster and easier than always printing out a new copy from the original computer file. We do keep the current handouts in a folder on our shared network space, so that any one of us can make a quick change to one of the handouts. Of course, we also have immediate access to all of our handouts on our Web site. Documents pertaining to citing sources, digital portfolio management, and database passwords are saved as PDFs and uploaded to our Web site with every change that we make. Find out what works best for your library squad and make it happen.

The other most common question was, "Can you recommend a good book? Or what should I read next?" We added links to our Web site that directed students to some of the better book-recommendation systems. We started by showing students how to use the book-recommendation system that is offered by one of our database providers. The system asks the user to enter a book that they like reading and then generates a report of other titles that the user may like based on some descriptive parameters. Several students experimented with these systems and reported back to us that they would much rather talk to us about book titles that we can guarantee that we have in our library. As we upgraded our online public access catalog (OPAC), we also found that we could steer users to an automated list within the graphical interface of our simple OPAC search. Most titles in the catalog now include a list of other titles that "you may also like." Numerous users shied away from these results, too, and said that they would prefer to talk to a real person about book recommendations. We were thrilled to get such honest feedback and are always happy to assist readers in book choices. In addition to this type of repetitive question being one of the best parts of being a librarian, we quickly learned that our users truly appreciated our input on this type of question.

Before you can recommend new book titles to a wide variety of library users, you need to actually read a lot of books. This is a challenge to anyone. Everyone is busy, but this has to be a priority item in your life if

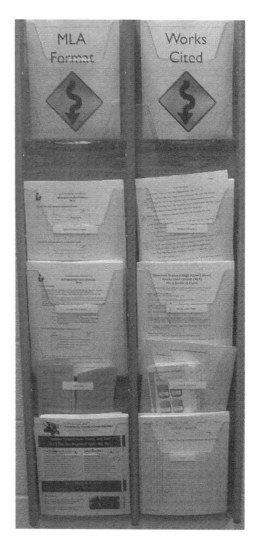

Figure 3.4.   Handouts

user-centered literacy is of any importance to you. We all read book reviews, but make sure that you are actually reading books and staying current with new titles. We owe it to our students to have honest recommendations in a variety of genres. Immerse yourself in the collections clamored for by your users. If you hear several users mention or request a specific title, take the time to read it and understand what it is that the users love about it. Is it the supernatural or the romance that appeals to so many students?

I'd like to add a note on "book talks." I have seen elementary school and children's librarians giving book talks to classes and small groups of students by imitating voices and really getting into the different characters of the books. While this is lovely for very young students, I prefer to keep book talks for high school students concise. Most high school students are not interested in hearing the history of the Holocaust in a five-minute book talk. They would prefer to hear that this book will make them cry or that they will learn a lot about World War II and the plight of the Gypsies in a 30-second book talk. Be compelling while still being appropriate for your users. Be sure to keep book talks brief, relevant, and not a lesson in historical fiction. Show your users how excited you are about the books and add some personal detail. We have noticed over and over again that the more you get your users to read and enjoy books, the more they will talk to their classmates about titles, and soon all users will come to rely on you for their next book recommendation. And by recommending books that you like to your users, you are creating lifelong readers by showing them how pleasurable reading can be.

Digital Portfolios

As our school now requires all students to create a digital portfolio in order to graduate, we also found ourselves answering tons of digital portfolio questions. We answered so many questions that we decided to create a special section in our library dedicated to the digital portfolio program. Our Digital Portfolio team created handouts and helped to train the library staff on all the intricacies of the program. We continue to answer questions about digital portfolios, but we all have consistent and standardized documentation to turn to when answering these questions, and students can move toward independent learning by understanding where to turn when they have future questions about the digital portfolio.

In addition to basic links and facts about digital portfolios, we created an online guide to our digital portfolio program so that students, faculty, and parents could refer to the information from home or school. Our online guide included a tab for each of our four classes (freshmen, sophomores, juniors, and seniors) as well as some basic information for parents and faculty to use. We incorporated deadlines, sample portfolios, rubrics, and checklists as well as several places where users could find additional information and training. This guide receives hundreds of views each month. It clearly illustrates two things to us: we had been repeatedly answering the same questions over and over again; and now students are able to access this information, plus more, via our online guide.

Another important aspect to everything we create online is to have a sense of humor. When writing sample student profiles for our guide, we decided to use a character from a 1990s sitcom instead of a serious example of a profile.

We also created a brochure that we could give to visitors, parents, teachers, and students who had questions on the details of a digital portfolio (Figure 3.5). The brochure explains the process, answers questions, and directs users where to find additional information. We always have plenty of copies available at open houses, conferences, and other public events in the library. (See Appendix C for Digital Portfolio handouts.)

Finally, we produced a simple-to-use checklist for the seniors to use as they approached this new graduation requirement. As the seniors were obviously worried about the new requirement, they repeatedly asked us how close they were to completion. We used simple language to create the checklist, and the students only need to check the yes or no columns in order to monitor their progress. We watch throughout the school year as students slowly move their checkmarks from the no column to the yes column.

Digital Portfolio Expectations	Yes	No
1 Do you have a written **student profile**?		
a. Is everything in your profile spelled correctly? Proper punctuation, grammar, capitalization used?		
b. Is there an image on your profile page?		
2 **Acquire Information:** Do you have 2 or more work samples in this folder?		
a. Does each work sample have a written reflection? (Which answers the following questions: What is it? What did you learn? Why did you put it in this section of your portfolio?)		
b. Is everything in the reflection spelled correctly? Proper punctuation, grammar, capitalization used?		
3 **Think Critically:** Do you have 2 or more work samples in this folder?		
a. Does each work sample have a written reflection? (Which answers the following questions: What is it? What did you learn? Why did you put it in this section of your portfolio?)		
b. Is everything in the reflection spelled correctly? Proper punctuation, grammar, capitalization used?		
4 **Communicate Effectively:** Do you have 2 or more work samples in this folder?		
a. Does each work sample have a written reflection? (Which answers the following questions: What is it? What did you learn? Why did you put it in this section of your portfolio?)		
b. Is everything in the reflection spelled correctly? Proper punctuation, grammar, capitalization used?		
5 **Perform Civic Duties:** Do you have 2 or more work samples in this folder?		
a. Does each work sample have a written reflection? (Which answers the following questions: What is it? What did you learn? Why did you put it in this section of your portfolio?)		
b. Is everything in the reflection spelled correctly? Proper punctuation, grammar, capitalization used?		

Figure 3.5.   Digital Portfolio Brochure

As we compiled the information for digital portfolios, one of our goals was to teach our students to be more independent in the creation and use of their digital portfolios. We do not have a specific class for students to take, so the information that we provide through the library is the only information that some of our students receive about it. We compiled the tools and resources in one place so that our students could be guided in the right direction. We have to demonstrate where to go to locate these resources, but once they find what they are looking for, they continue to return. We also do this in the hopes that students will turn to our Web site and guides for other new and more complex information retrieval situations. We have given them experiential context for locating information that they need. They must extrapolate that information and eventually intuitively move in the right direction for additional information needs.

Just-in-Case Instruction

I am not a fan of just-in-case instruction of any sort. Herding freshmen into the library for lessons on how to use databases and conduct research is not the way to prevent students from asking repetitive questions. In fact, we have found that students often feel that their time spent in the library in one of these classes is a waste and shows to them how confusing, complicated, and irrelevant the library actually is.

If you want to instruct students on how to use the library databases, the online catalog, or other resources in your library, wait for them to actually need the instruction. Just-in-time instruction means collaborating with faculty members on new research projects, being sure that all students in all sections of a subject are receiving similar topics at similar times, and keeping track of what information skills have not been covered. When you notice that a topic is not being covered, be sure to locate a willing faculty member and sneak it into one of their upcoming research projects. Just be sure to teach the skill or resource in the context that it is needed.

For example, when you notice that students are repeatedly asking for more information on creating a properly formatted MLA header or in-text citation, approach a teacher with whom you enjoy working and find out what their next project will be. Suggest to the teacher that the students begin the lesson in the library, where you can show students how to create the properly formatted header using your local word-processing tool. You can also walk the students through a lesson on citing their textbook and include a perfectly formatted in-text citation within a paragraph. Research the actual process first, practice the lesson on your own, and take a few notes. I also like to look into alternative ways of doing something. With most word-processing tools, there are several ways to do almost everything. It is definitely a good idea to have a few ways to share with students with different learning styles. Some like mouse clicks while others prefer shortcut keys. I am frequently surprised by the number of times in which someone shows me something that I have been doing for years one way and they have a completely new and viable way of doing it. Reach out to your users occasionally and ask for their favorite shortcuts.

If your users are asking the same questions over and over again, they may be having a frustrating experience in your library. Continue to monitor repetitive questions and find new ways to assist your users. We also think about the users who do not ask questions. Perhaps by creating some of the handouts, signs, and online guides and by rearranging the placement of resources and supplies, you can help those users find more of the information and resources that they need. You will find unexpected and simple solutions to some of your most frustrating repeat offenders.

Your To-Do List

✓ Collect a list of questions for a week. Check off how many times you answer the same question.

✓ Brainstorm ideas for dealing with those questions that you answer several times.

✓ Consider moving items that are requested often to the most obvious location for your users.

✓ ($) Order signs to label four or five major areas in a one-room library.

✓ Label book stacks with aisle or shelf numbers.

✓ Create simple handouts for frequently asked questions.

✓ ($) Establish a single, well-labeled location where handouts can be retrieved.

✓ Be sure that everyone on your library squad has electronic access to the original handouts and to your Web presence—so that anyone can make a change or update.

4

Step Four: Join Resources

One of the central themes to creating an information commons is creating a collaborative and central portal where access to information of all sorts is located. Create a single centralized information hub where faculty, staff, and students gather to find out almost anything that they need to know. Create a space for one-stop shopping for information, tools, and resources available at your school or on your campus.

One of the most common things to do when creating a learning commons is to collaborate with or integrate the library with the technology help desk, the technology integrator, and/or the technology director (as shown in Figure 4.1). We did not plan to merge or combine our departments, creating one. We still wanted to have separate entities, just working side by side in the library to benefit all of our users. A big part in beginning this step is educating your administration and technology department. Invite librarians from local learning commons to speak to you and your technology people about how they joined resources. Share articles, blogs, and e-mails with your technology department and administration about the trend in a shift towards the learning commons model. Handing an entire book, like this one, to a technology department or administrator may be too much information at once. Perhaps you will stand a better chance by highlighting passages and marking pages specifically pertinent to your library program.

Talk to the administration about joining resources with those departments. Every school and library operates differently, but one easy and inexpensive thing that most institutions can make happen is to establish a common meeting time for the librarians and the technology professionals. Also share some of the high-touch tasks for which your technology people are not available in the middle of a busy school day. Talk to the technology administrators about the ease and ability to reset student passwords, access student network folders, retrieve lost documents on the network, and access blocked Web sites.

In small schools and libraries across the country, the library is already the place to interact one-on-one with research librarians, technology experts, and media specialists because all of these duties are delivered by one individual. Keep this in mind when thinking about creating your own learning commons. You may already be doing a large philosophical shift that is difficult to make happen in larger schools and libraries.

Technology administrators are usually in charge of filtering the access to information. While they are perfectly qualified to filter access from a compliant standpoint, you could argue that a librarian has more expertise in determining the quality of that access as it relates to academics and research. This shift is an important one, and something that could be done today. Go to your administration and explain that you are the trained

Figure 4.1.   Technology Team

professional in areas of access to relevant information. Public schools and libraries that accept government e-rate money are required to filter the Internet, due to the Children's Internet Protection Act (CIPA) laws, but there are no laws about who should be in charge of selecting the resources that are blocked. We work together with our technology staff in blocking and allowing access to information via the Web. Oftentimes, the technology administrators feel more like gatekeepers, blocking access to what they believe to be inappropriate materials. The technology administrators are frequently driven by fear

Figures 4.2a   Student/Technology Interaction

Figures 4.2b   Student/Technology Interaction

and protection rather than pedagogy. Librarians, on the other hand, are usually gate openers. We are the professionals in a building looking for ways to provide the most people with the most information. It makes sense to me that librarians should be involved in a large part of content filtering.

Simply adding more computers to your library space does not make an information commons. Adding more computers because your users need them to meet their academic needs may be a part of your shift. However, the more important aspect is working together with the technology individuals that support your library. Share knowledge, tools, training, resources, and ideas between the departments (Figures 4.2a and 4.2b). The technology department is rarely interacting with learners as much as the library squad is. Be sure to keep them informed of what all of your users are asking for and talking about.

If you and your library squad are granted some level of technology administration, not only are you interfacing with users more often, but you are reinforcing the learning commons model in action by being the go-to resource for basic technology questions and problems. Also, by working closely with the technology department, you will have another level of professional in the building invested in making the learning commons model more successful. Together, we will be able to help our users with their information needs better that if we were helping them on our own.

One way to see which resources or services need to work together is to track unmonitored referrals. Keep track of anytime a user asks you a question that requires you to send the user out of the library. Volunteer to manage additional equipment or perform additional functions such as resetting passwords or giving out SAT test information. Discuss with administration about including these locations, resources, and equipment in the new information commons area. Students are coming to you and expecting that you can help them with their computer logins and registering for standardized tests, so why not gather those resources together and actually answer the questions, instead of sending students off to the technology help desk or the guidance department for some of these simple requests?

Questions to Ask Yourself

- Does your school need a library when most information can be accessed in the classroom using the Internet?
- What is it that your library offers to your user in addition to accessing information?
- Could you manage any additional functions or information in order to become more valuable to your school?
- Do you have more than one location within your library where users can ask questions? If so, do they have different uses?

Most large-sized libraries have multiple information desks in one library. Consider combining those library services (ILL, checkouts, and reference) into one help desk. If your users have one place, possibly staffed by different people, to go to anytime they have a question about anything, they will feel more comfortable approaching the desk and asking a question. One desk to answer all questions is the perfect illustration of simplicity for users.

Personal Learning Networks

Join with other libraries in your district, school administrative unit, region, state, and nationwide. Librarians all over the world love to share information and resources. The librarians of your local district may meet monthly to discuss sharing assets, but the most valuable thing that you can share with each other is ideas. Make sure to meet with other professional librarians monthly. If you are having trouble with a specific issue, you can guarantee that several other librarians are dealing with the same issue.

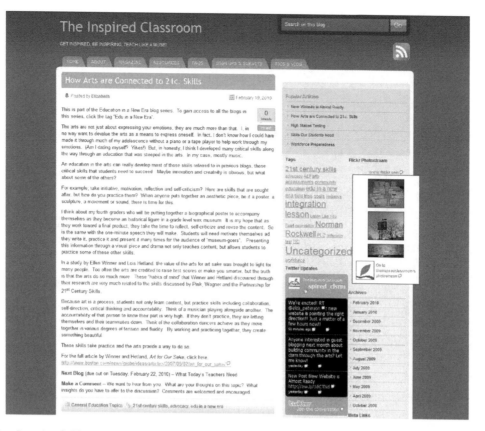

Figure 4.3.   Inspired Classroom Social Network

As an active member in a professional librarian association, you can offer to work at a conference in exchange for free admission to the conference. In addition to attending the conference and working at it, you will also have the added pleasure of getting to meet hundreds of other friendly librarians.

Stay in touch with all of your library colleagues by following them on micro-blogging and information resource–sharing systems (such as that in Figure 4.3). Create a group in a social networking site and invite your fellow librarians to join. If you join resources with like-minded librarians from around the world, you will always have an incubator for new ideas and a powerful support network when the new ideas are not flowing freely. Try finding some colleagues from around the world to join up with. Watch how conversations develop and keep track of how other users respond. Each service and system has its own benefits and specialties. Be sure to try out a few different systems, and do not just stick with one, until you find the one that works best for you.

The Plymouth Model

At our school, we decided to mash up the library and the technology department in an unofficial way. We have the administrator from the technology department serve as our liaison to the administration team meetings. Our technology coordinator also attends our monthly staff meetings, is included on library department e-mails, and is informed of problems, new ideas, and any new information from the library staff. In addition, we also attempt to talk in person every day. We don't always cross paths on a daily basis, but it is our unofficial goal to speak or stay in contact every day.

As we were first beginning to join resources, we moved 40 computers and a networked printer into the library. Because the library suddenly became the largest computer lab in the school, we found that we needed to communicate more frequently. As more users filtered into the library for technology-related issues, we continued to see what they needed and offered them solutions. As we added the computers over the years, we also added USB drives, digital cameras, digital video cameras, digital voice recorders, netbooks, electronic book readers, and micro-card readers. Soon, when any user had a technology-related question, they called the library. We became the driving force behind allowing students to use portable devices for storing and sharing information. We pushed for open access to resources such as video-sharing Web sites, micro-blogging services, and e-mail for all students. Simply opening the lines of communication between the library and the technology department allowed many of our initiatives to come to fruition.

When communicating with the technology department, be sure to do your research first, and then explain that your needs are driven by the needs of your users. When we requested a color printer for the library, it was not because the library squad was hoping to print out our reports in color, although that is a benefit for us. Instead, we explained that several science reports, data charts, and art projects were requiring color printouts. Students were unable to print out a draft of a digital art project in color before they sent their projects through the art teacher's high-resolution printer. Teachers were unable to print out data charts with different color labels for each data set without a color printer. We researched color printers using consumer comparison Web sites, we did ink-refill-cost comparisons, and asked colleagues via a micro-blogging service. We gathered all of our information together and went to the technology department with our requests, our research, and our examples of why our users needed a color printer available in the library. They couldn't say no. The following summer, we had a new color printer, and our users were able to use it on the first day of school.

Auxiliary Faculty

The administration, seeing that we were the leaders in technology across the school, decided to move the digital portfolio coordinator to under the umbrella of the library. In the state of New Hampshire, every student must collect and reflect on their digital artifacts of learning into a digital portfolio. We knew that students were already using the library to develop inquiry, create knowledge, and experiment with technology, so why not provide space and resources specifically for collecting and reflecting on their learning through the use of digital portfolios? We thought that it made sense for students and faculty to have a place within the school where they could ask questions, access resources, and share information. In order to do this, we created an area near the computers in the library for a "Digital Portfolio" help desk. In addition to sharing brochures, FAQs, checklists, and rubrics, we also became the repository for the student passwords. Students began stopping first in our library for all levels of digital portfolio assistance. Our library became the digital portfolio center for our school (Figure 4.4).

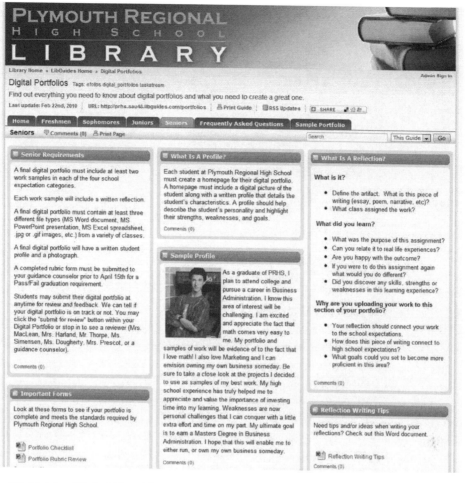

Figure 4.4.   LibGuides Digital Portfolio

We also saw that students were asking for some very specific assistance in the areas of math, English, and language arts. We changed our library duty position, the person who used to check passes, into a library tutor. We ordered a professionally designed laminate sign for the library, moved two more desks into the library under the sign, and seated our new tutors at these desks. Faculty members now write library passes specifically for working with tutors, and as students sign into the library, they are directed to the tutoring stations. We now have full-time tutors available to help with rewriting papers, citing sources, and coming up with thesis statements (some of the most time-consuming and highly specialized English-specific questions that are asked in the library). Furthermore, students now have live and personalized assistance with math homework, math software guidance, and even statistical analysis support. The library staff is highly trained in assisting students with specialized information and technology resources; but we were never prepared to answer mathematics questions, and those questions would usually result in an unmonitored referral outside of the library. If you are fortunate enough to provide specialized tutoring in your library, be sure to keep statistics on the number of service interactions between tutors and users. These statistics will be invaluable to the administration at budget time.

Figure 4.5.   Library Squad

Proceed with the goal that you are building an elite library squad. Surround yourself with the people who are proactive and eager to learn. We found that when were hiring a new paraprofessional in the library, we all benefitted from hiring a technology aide rather than an aide more experienced in libraries. An aide already trained in technology, especially resources-sharing technologies, is a valuable hire. We found that people with existing library experience often had their own prejudices to extinguish before they could accurately understand the goals that we had established for our library in our shift toward a learning commons.

Another important element in looking for an addition to your library squad is to hire well-rounded, educated people (our squad appears in Figure 4.5). We find it crucial to have members of our team know that a student is looking for *the Divine Comedy* and not a nineties sci-fi film about volcanoes when they ask for "Dante's Inferno." Once again, while it is possible to teach your library squad how to update the library catalog, set up a scanner, and import sound files from a digital voice recorder, it is extremely difficult to teach an "unsocial" person how to be people-oriented. Adding well-educated and social individuals to your library squad will help your team to work together to make a better learning commons.

I have noticed in all my years of working in and visiting a variety of libraries that sometimes librarians are not always the best "salespeople." In fact, I have heard librarians say that they went to library school because they liked books more than people or that they specifically did not have anything to sell. Unfortunately, due to budget restraints and the availability of mobile information, administrators are looking at all areas within their organizations for cuts. Librarians do have something very serious to sell. We have our expertise at selecting appropriate resources, locating difficult-to-find information, teaching information literacy, and so much more. At school and academic libraries, we also have the task of teaching our users how to find their own information. We all must sell our skills to our users, faculty, administration, school boards, trustees, and the community. We need to constantly prove our value to the stakeholders. Perhaps you feel reluctant or apprehensive about these changes, but your ideas, actions, and policy implementation are probably the things that give your library the most value.

Community Resources

In addition to joining resources with other departments, be sure to join resources with other libraries, librarians, professional organizations, historical societies, and other information resources in your community. Some of the best, and least expensive, professional development opportunities are visits to surrounding libraries. Take a look at Web sites, follow discussions on the local library organizations listservs, and do a little research. Even libraries that you think you know all about are apt to surprise you with a hidden and valuable gem of an idea.

Join your local professional organizations. Volunteer to write for the organization's newsletter or weblog. Share ideas on the listservs, too. One of the most beneficial ways to get involved is to dive right in and volunteer to assist the planning committee of a local conference. People are always thrilled to have an extra pair of hands during an overwhelming conference week. You will also get to meet lots of like-minded librarians, probably attend the conference for free, and learn a little something along the way.

For years, libraries have been sharing MARC records through copy cataloging. Find new ways to share resources with librarians from all over the world. It will be a gratifying solution to problems you didn't know you had.

Look at other library Web sites and look to ways of joining together for Web site inspiration and redesign. E-mail the librarians responsible for the Web sites and ask for some basic directions and permission to use some of their ideas. At Plymouth, we often look at the local university Web sites. Think about the tools that your users will be using when they leave your library. Can you make any changes to your Web presence to begin educating your users about more complex Web resources that they may need in the future? We are lucky enough to have a university in our town. The faculty at Plymouth State University has been extremely generous in sharing ideas and resources with everyone at our high school.

We have also been thinking about guiding students in the creation of their own personal learning networks. Who are the people they want to be in contact with? Once your professional learning network is established, imagine how you can share that information and experience with your learners. Schedule a time at a faculty meeting to briefly demonstrate how you use micro-blogging, RSS feeds, and listservs. Once the faculty is using their professional learning networks, they will encourage students to do the same. Students can make connections between faculty members, fellow students, and learners out in the world that they have not met face to face.

Your To-Do List

✓ Get your technology department on board with your library shift.

✓ Brainstorm ideas for joining resources in your own building.

✓ Join library listservs; sign up to receive RSS feeds about several library blogs.

✓ Share your successes with other librarians.

✓ Ask yourself: What does our library do that nobody else on campus can do?

✓ ($) Create a highly specialized, educated, well-rounded, user-focused, and elite library squad.

✓ Visit local libraries for your next professional development day.

✓ Share your knowledge and resource lists with the community (especially crucial at budget time).

From *The Learning Commons: Seven Simple Steps to Transform Your Library* by Pamela Colburn Harland. Santa Barbara, CA: Libraries Unlimited. Copyright © 2011.

5

Step Five: Remove Barriers

Physical Barriers

Put the tools and resources that your users need on the other side of the counter and then get rid of the counter. It is one of the most difficult steps, but once you open your locked cabinets to your users, you will spend a lot less time handing out glue sticks and yearbooks and more time teaching information literacy and collaborating with faculty.

I know how safe it feels to stand behind the counter. It strongly represents a barrier, protecting the library staff and everything else that sits behind the counter from the users. The shift here is to change your philosophy from protecting resources and materials to guiding your users. When I was in graduate school, we were still studying preservation and archiving of print collections. This is part of the long-standing library legacy that we have learned and used for centuries. The problem exists when we extend those feelings of preservation and protection to resources such as glue sticks.

Through informal research, we found that users of all kinds felt that a counter-level desk or any other kind of large furniture, was uninviting. Users feel intimidated to approach it. Students relate it to a judge's bench in a courtroom, the main desk at a police station, or a teller's counter at a bank. Our students are not comfortable approaching these unfamiliar places, and they extended that feeling to our library information desk. Users feel like they have to ask the question the right way, even when they do not necessarily know what the question is. We tried to make our counter inviting, adding decorations, displaying free bookmarks, and seating student workers behind it, but our users continued to be put off by our high desk. They felt like they were being judged by those of us behind the counter.

We designed a welcoming low desk with some surrounding counters as our main desk as in Figure 5.1. We wanted to be sure that students did not feel that they could help themselves to parts of the desk, as we frequently have books that have not yet been checked in, or materials on reserve for other users on our desk. However, the part of the desk where the students approach, either to ask questions or to check out materials, is low and inviting.

I also continue to find a lot of valuable resources behind every librarian's desk that I have visited. More often than not, office supplies are located behind the desk. I completely understand the need to guard the supplies against waste and reckless use. But I guarantee that the day you put the supplies on the other side of the desk is the day that you suddenly have more time to spend on innovative ideas, collaboration with faculty, and facilitating information literacy with the students in your library. Some

Figure 5.1. Checkout Desk

libraries keep dictionaries, popular book titles (like the *Guinness Book of World Records*), the *MLA Handbook*, the *World Almanac*, school yearbooks, audiobooks, and other highly desired and valuable resources behind the desk. These resources are for the users, not for the protecting. Librarians are worried about theft, destruction, and inappropriate use of these materials. I encourage you to buy extra copies of the materials that are overused or too popular to actually trust in the hands of a student. Take a chance by shifting how you share resources with your users.

Emotional Barriers

Not all barriers are physical barriers. I am not a "touchy-feely" kind of gal, but I have seen that in addition to high counters, people often put up emotional barriers. Some librarians, including myself on the most frantic days, give off the vibe of being too busy to talk. They have their heads buried behind their monitor with the obvious message of "Don't talk to me; I am too busy for you." No user wants to ever hear how busy you are. The library squad should not be displaying leisure, but a library is not a place for panic and stress, either. Most of us have an unending job to do behind that computer monitor, so I have several suggestions for how to be more approachable.

When I first introduce myself to students, I explain to them that they are welcome to come into my office whenever they have a question for me. I warn them that I may look busy, because most of the time I am working on my computer. I assure them that I would much rather be talking to them than working on my computer, so I encourage them to interrupt me, no matter how seriously busy I look at my computer. I also need to remind myself periodically that I told students this, as sometimes it is frustrating to be constantly disrupted. But, when we are trying to establish a culture of open collaboration and innovative facilitation, I need to be able to set aside my frustration, especially for our student users.

I have experienced the frightening experience of approaching the larger-than-life reference desk, asking for assistance on a research topic, getting a look over the glasses by the intimidating librarian on the other side of the desk who invariably asks, "Have you looked it up?" That is such a menacing, but all too common, experience for a young student or uninitiated library user. If a user is asking you for help, take the time to show them what they need. Please be sure to think of the negative experiences that you have had (or heard about) in a library or other information desk–type location and avoid duplication in your library. One of the most beneficial things that you can do is to create a space without these types of barriers. Fear, intimidation, and trepidation are adjectives that should not be associated with your library space. Try to put yourself in your users' positions and think of how you would like to be treated. You are there for them.

I have seen signs on librarian's desks that say things like, "Please interrupt me." I imagine that users appreciate the invitation to approach a professional sitting at a desk behind a computer, seemingly engrossed in a project that is more important than you. Take the time to think of alternative ways that you can take down invisible barriers, too.

Working with Faculty

We attracted faculty to the library in a number of ways. We were never too busy to talk to a faculty member who walked into our office. If they want to talk and they are coming to you, make the time to welcome them and help them to feel included in decisions happening at the library. Insisting that teachers make appointments, fill out forms, or happen to stop by when you have nothing at all to do is a huge barrier for busy faculty members. You may have to increase staffing in order to be able to triage your user's needs, so that you always have time to talk to all of your users.

Another way in which we attracted faculty into the library is by always having a jar of chocolate available to them (Figure 5.2). Several times each day, we have faculty and staff stopping by for a chocolate break. Frequently, while they grab a handful of candy, our conversation turns from casual greetings to collaboration on a project. If a teacher mentions a research project that is coming up, I will gather print and online resources for them, offer our library to their classes, put books on reserve for their project, and follow up with an e-mail. After two years of forcing myself onto our faculty, and not letting up, I now have most of the faculty stopping by at the first thought of a research project. The library has become the place that teachers can rely on for providing valuable resources as well as information-literacy lessons to their students.

We do not force teachers to fill out forms in order to schedule a class visit or a collaboration meeting in the library. We find that teachers have too much going on. If we want them to utilize the librarian's skills and our resources, then we must remove barriers such as forms and other unnecessary administrative steps that we used to insist faculty jump through. If a teacher calls, stops by, or sends an e-mail about an upcoming research project, we do our best to prepare the library for them. We currently have a

Figure 5.2.   Chocolate

paper calendar that we use as the library scheduling tool. It is extremely low-tech, but it is the best tool for us to keep track of our calendar and upcoming research projects and class visits. We have considered making it available on our Web site or our shared network space so that teachers could be constantly informed of our schedule, but we have not moved in that direction for several reasons:

1. We prefer to have teachers come into the library when signing up for time with us. This offers us the opportunity to discuss projects, needs, and tools with the teachers.
2. When between classes, it is faster for us to look down at the binder on the desk rather than check a computer.
3. It is flexible, as we only write in pencil, but it is also easy to track changes and make notes regarding class size, resource requirements, research projects, and lesson ideas.

Encourage the rest of your library squad to increase their social interactions, especially if you have new staff working in the library. We encourage our staff to eat lunch in the staff room or the cafeteria, attend meetings, and attend after-school activities such as football games, school plays, and award ceremonies. This removes a barrier of not actually knowing who it is that works in the library. We want our library squad to be social and approachable, and we want people to know who they are when they walk into the library. Making an effort to connect with our patrons encourages them to develop a relationship with us that will increase the likelihood that they will use our services and materials and support the library when it comes to budget time. We make it a priority to be an integrated member of the staff.

Virtual Barriers

Virtual barriers are much easier to deal with. Users often cannot access online resources due to password protection, incompatible Web browsers or specific software requirements, unnecessary technology complexity, and lack of access to technology.

In order to provide access to one of your most vital resources, a user must be able to access your online databases and electronic resources. Your subscription resources must be password protected, but you should provide a simple way to remotely access the password list. Supply your users with a single easy-to-remember password and create a Web page that contains all of your online resource passwords in one simple form. Password-protect that page and you have restricted access to only those users who know the password to the password page. Users now have a key to all of our passwords and links. We used a free wiki page to do this very easily (Figure 5.3). Several blogging tools, wiki tools, and course management programs offer a password-protected option.

Be sure to create MARC records for any electronic resources that you have and create flexible search terms. This will remind your users to utilize your databases even when they were expecting to find a traditional print resource. MARC records can be downloaded from the database vendors and include a link directly to the resource. We found that this increased the use of several databases the month that we included the MARC records in our library catalog. Some of our large database vendors send a MARC record for every periodical title, reference book, biography, and map collection held in their collection. Now, if a user searches for a newspaper that you have available only via a database vendor, that paper comes up as an "electronic resource" with a link directly to the title within the database. Users still need passwords, so education on the location of passwords is crucial, especially for users doing their searching off site, as IP authentication is sometimes attached to your database account.

Figure 5.3.   Accessing Databases

A Note to Database Vendors and Electronic Resource Providers

I am sure it is the hope of all librarians that database vendors and electronic resource providers will agree on some standardized or customizable search standard that will make all electronic resources as user friendly and easy to use as the rest of our libraries. We are looking toward simplicity, customizability, and user-centered design.

Some electronic resources require a special reader to be installed on the computer. We shy away from any resource like this—we find that the software, even if it is free, is often complicated; updates need to be loaded periodically; and students are forbidden from adding new software to any school computers. This prevents students from being able to access some of our online resources, even from computers in the school library. Frustrating! Most electronic resources are now available in any Web browser, but before you purchase anything new, be sure to ask questions about access. The lesson here is to stay away from proprietary electronic resources, use a basic Web browser as the tool as most users have free and existing access already to a simple Web browser.

Much like the special readers for electronic resources, several audiobook and e-book suppliers create proprietary interfaces. In order to better serve your patrons, be sure to purchase audiobooks and e-books that your users are looking for. If you provide hardware in your library for listening to or reading these resources, be sure to purchase the resources that your users are looking for. Do some research, interview your users, and create a survey before investing in equipment or subscriptions to these tools. You do not want to create a barrier to new resources while you are attempting to provide greater access.

Another important way to remove virtual barriers is to approach your users wherever they are. Be sure to ask your users about what tools they most commonly use—social networking, micro-blogging, regular blogs through RSS feeds, instant messaging, texting, other specific Web sites, etc. Once you find out which tools are most commonly being used, sign up for them.

The Plymouth Model

In addition to having our own social networking pages, blogs, photo-sharing, and micro-blogging accounts, we also set up PRHS Library accounts. We constantly keep a list of blogging and micro-blogging ideas to use for future posts. We set up a simple word-processing document on our network shared space, so that everyone on the library squad has access to it. Throughout the school year, we all can share ideas on this simple document. When it comes time to start a new issue of our newsletter or we feel the need to add a new blog entry, we open the document and scan through our ideas to find one that is relevant and meaningful.

Every time we have an event in the library (for example, an author visit, Banned Books Week, Teen Read Week, etc.) we promote it through micro-blogging and on our social networking pages (Figure 5.4). Once it is over, we document it through our photo-sharing and blog tools. We also like to acknowledge new standout books that arrive in the library, an occasional author's birthday celebration, and school-wide

Figure 5.4.   PRHS Blog Entry

events like Homecoming, school elections, and Winter Carnival. We make every attempt to keep our writing conversational, approachable, and inviting so that all users will want to keep coming back to our tools. Once we are approachable in our virtual worlds, users will feel more comfortable approaching us via e-mail and in person, too.

When we remodeled our Web presence, we made sure that in addition to creating a user-friendly and flexible Web site, any and all barriers were removed. We tried to use simple design, plenty of white space, images, and inviting tools to create an approachable, low-counter design to our Web site. We included several widgets with direct links to our photo-sharing account, micro-blogging account, and online version of our statistics and newsletter. We wanted to make sure that everything we do would be readily accessible from this one virtual space. We do not want to have any barriers between our users and the online information that we provide to them. Creating a confusing or complicated Web site is just like putting print resources that your users need to use in a locked-up room.

Even though we spend a lot of our time meeting with classes and introducing them to our online databases, we want to make sure that the online information is

Figure 5.5.   Mobile Learning

accessible to any user that needs access. We do not want any barriers around our information or around the services that we provide.

Personalizing Information Resources

Personalizing information technologies, utilizing student-owned devices, is an important aspect of the future of learning commons. Allow students to add any updates to the Web site or resource guides to their own personal learning space. As you consider making changes to your Web presence, think about how learners will receive updates. Do they need to go to your Web site, or can your Web site go to them? If you are making updates via a blogging tool, be sure to add RSS feeds as a sharing option. As we update one of our research guides, any user who signs up for it can receive an e-mail update, an aggregator update via RSS feed, or a micro-blogging tweet.

Several databases are providing a space for learners to share their own book ratings and reviews. Be sure to turn this feature on and encourage your users to join in on the book-talking fun. You may want to encourage your English teachers to offer a bit of extra credit for every book review added to the library catalog.

We are also encouraging our administration to change some policies in the student handbook. We want students to be able to utilize their own Web-enabled devices at our school (such as those in Figure 5.5), but will settle for access within the library. Using student-owned devices such as smartphones, netbooks, and laptops with updates to the resources that they need is creating a user's own mobile learning commons. Your users are self-directed and empowered with their own customized information being sent directly to them.

In addition to removing any virtual barriers, we also took the time to remove physical barriers. We were fortunate to be able to redesign our checkout desk. We created a much smaller unit in the front corner of the library. We removed a huge barrier of a counter with bookshelves in front of it that expanded all the way across the front of the library. Our barrier prevented most users from accessing supplies, videos, the professional collection, and equipment. It also created a solid division between "us" and "them." With this one project, we created an open atmosphere in the library that cannot be undone. We removed the "fortress" that served as the main desk.

With very few changes, visitors now come in to the library and exclaim that the library is very open and inviting. People did not say that when visitors walked in and were surrounded on both sides by a counter-level checkout desk that expanded all the way across the front of the library. Look at your library and see what barriers are created by the arrangement of furniture and the height of information desks. In particular, look at the location of your desk. Are you approachable? Do all users feel that you are an accessible part of the library? Is your Web presence adaptable for your users? Pick one thing that you want to change, and do it today.

Your To-Do List

✓ Change one thing that you can change today!

✓ Look at what you keep behind your desk. Move it to a high-traffic area for easy access and high visibility.

✓ Toss out "collaboration" forms and start collaborating more often with teachers.

✓ ($) Buy a bag of M&Ms and send an e-mail to the faculty about chocolate-filled collaboration breaks in the library.

✓ ($) If you currently sit behind a counter, look for ways that you can lower that counter.

✓ Make your desk more approachable for faculty and students.

✓ Encourage your library squad to eat lunch in the teacher break room, attend more meetings, and go watch school events. Social interaction creates a more approachable library staff.

✓ Personalize services.

✓ Create a password-protected Web page with access to electronic resources.

✓ Reach out to users in whatever tools they most commonly use.

6

Step Six: Trust Your Users

You purchase the materials for your users, so give up a little more control and trust them with access to supplies, equipment, reference books and yearbooks as well as virtual spaces.

When you create an atmosphere of trust, your users will be more likely to approach you for a larger variety of information and services. Americans in general have created this strange new atmosphere of entitlement. What librarian has not heard a user explain, "I returned that book!" in frustration for both parties. I am not recommending that you trust everything that your users claim. I am suggesting that we trust that they believe, or are at least hopeful that whatever they claim is the truth. We assume that our users have good intentions. We do not need to have overly permissive attitudes towards our users, but let's also not move towards the other extreme of constantly saying "no" to our users. It is a steady balancing act between what is appropriate and what is possible. Provide a service to your users, not a test.

One rule that I feel strongly about is the frequently held policy that restricts students from being able to check out an unlimited number of resources from the library. Your resources are purchased for your users. Why not allow them unlimited access, especially to the books (Figure 6.1)? I know that I often have a steady stream of 5–10 library books at my house at any given time. Sometimes I'm in the mood for some professional development, sometimes I want to read a young adult mystery, and other times I am hankering for a good old graphic novel. Show your users that you trust them by allowing them to check out as many books as they want. Just because you are worried about a small number of users who will keep their materials for too long—or worse, lose them—you can trust most of your users with a more liberal policy allowing unrestricted access to your print resources.

Providing students with a wide variety of resources is only one part of creating an information commons. The space that you create must be filled with open collaboration and an open exchange of ideas. In order for this atmosphere to come to fruition, the users must be acknowledged, and librarians can respect their users by trusting them.

Virtual Trust

Show your users that you trust them by allowing them access to your Web presence. Allow—no, encourage—your users to leave comments on your Web site. Ask faculty and students to share links on a wiki or your research guides (Figure 6.2). Create Web sites with open access for your community members to participate. When you are introducing the library Web site to a new group of users, show the

Figure 6.1.   No Limits on Borrowing Books

students how to add resources to the existing pages. Allow users to go in and share their ideas with the rest of the class. Explain to them that you trust them, that you expect them to use these resources responsibly, and that you value their ideas and opinions. This helps to create the open and collaborative environment of a true information commons.

Most new online public access catalogs now include a section where users can comment on and review library materials. Turn this option on and see how much your users want to share their opinions about what they are reading with the rest of the community. Facilitate this by serving as a model and reviewing all of the books that you read, too. In addition, make it easy for users to sign in to your catalog by creating easy to remember usernames and passwords. User contribution is a great way to see how your students are using your resources.

Continually lobby for your users to have access to digital resources like video sharing, photo sharing, e-mail, blogging, micro-blogging, and social networking. We

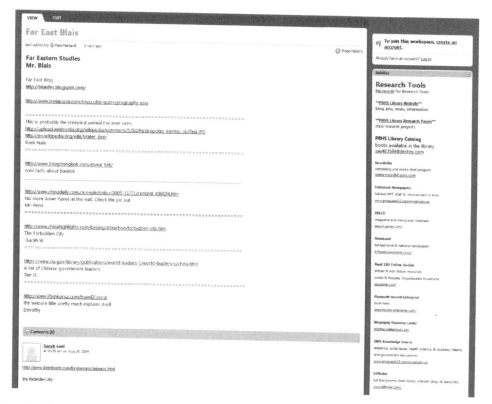

Figure 6.2.   Students Using the Wiki

are constantly reevaluating our accessible-use policy and looking how to change the language to make it more of a flexible and trusting document for our users, while at the same time protecting the school's network and liability issues. Demonstrate to your students how to responsibly use these resources as part of their civic duties in a digital world. Instead of blocking access to them, trust that they will learn to use these resources responsibly with the help of a reasonable role model.

A lot of schools have social networking policies forbidding faculty from being "friends" with students. This policy is based on distrust of how a professional teacher would use a social networking tool. Some teachers themselves have a policy against "friending" students until they graduate. I am fully supportive of whatever policy you want to create for yourself. However, if our students do not have mentors in the area of social networking, blogging, micro-blogging, and other online behaviors, where will they learn how to be a responsible member of the digital society we have created? I recommend allowing students to join your social networking circles, but constantly thinking about how your use of these tools is serving as a teaching opportunity for these students. Like any other digital environment, do not ever post anything that you wouldn't want your mother, boss, or a student to see. Even if you have no student followers on your micro-blog, those status reports never actually go away. Be sure to always keep your digital life professional, and to have enough trust in yourselves and in your colleagues that you would encourage the staff at your school to allow students into your social networking lives.

Take student requests seriously. When a student requests a book title, a piece of software, or a new technology tool, you need to take this as critical information.

If one student has the nerve to request materials from the library, you can safely assume that several others would like to utilize the same resources, but did not specifically ask you. Trusting student requests is a great place to begin shifting your current library into a user-centered, collaborative learning commons.

In addition to advocating for access to digital resources, with every book that you decide not to purchase and add to your collection, you are making a decision on whether or not your users have access to print information and resources. A lot of librarians feel the need to protect their users from dangerous information in books about witchcraft, homosexuality, drug use, and other notorious topics. We all need to continually evaluate whether or not we are the biggest book banners in our library by simply deciding not to purchase specific titles on controversial topics.

The Kindle Learning Commons

During the summer of 2009, I was asked to speak to a group of school administrators about how we are accessing information in our library and where I thought that the future of the library was heading. As I prepared for my presentation, I thought a lot about personalizing information and education services for each student, providing more mobility in our learning environment, and continuing to develop our library from an old-fashioned legacy-modeled book room into a user-centered learning commons. I wanted to show the administrators how portable and instant access to information could be in this future library, so I spent a good deal of time showing them e-books.

We were currently subscribing to several large databases that were filled with electronic reference books. We rarely purchase print reference books anymore, as it is so much easier for our users to access the constantly updated information via a single database search. We weeded our reference collection of everything that was now accessible via our online databases and saved dozens of shelves. What library couldn't use a little bit more space for books?

We had also received a collection of classic e-books from our online public access catalog that readers could access from anywhere that they had Internet access. Students could now access a copy of *Hamlet* from their laptop at home through a simple search in our library catalog.

We had been considering purchasing a collection of literary criticism in e-book format, but the search tool was a separate tool altogether. In order for our students to access all of these e-books, they had to search in several different online resources. We found this frustrating and difficult to teach. Our students were already confused about where to turn for the best information, so I was not interested in adding one more option to the already large list of options. We were hoping to find a simpler tool to lend to our students so that they could access hundreds of e-books at once. During the spring of 2009, we had several requests from students asking if we going to purchase Amazon Kindles for our library, and we thought that this might be the answer.

During the presentation to the school administrators, I showed them images of young people using Kindles at the beach, in a park, and at a desk in a library. I explained that the Kindle DX can hold 3,500 books, it weighs one pound, it can read the book out loud to a user, and it includes a built-in dictionary.

I was contacted by one of the administrators a few weeks later. She had asked me to pick out my dream Kindle and include accessories. I picked out a skin, a case, an extra power cord, an extended warranty, and the newest Kindle. She wrote a grant, and three months later, 20 brand-new Kindles, cases, power cords, skins, warranties, and gift cards for titles showed up at my library.

I sent desperate messages out on the listservs asking for advice on managing Kindles in our library. I tweeted several pleas for help or advice on what our library policies should be. I heard crickets chirping in response. I felt protective of these new and expensive devices. I was afraid to make any decision until we had rock-solid policies in place.

We decided to sign the Kindles out to the elite library squad: the library staff, digital portfolio coordinator, the technology department, and a number of English and social studies teachers. We added several titles, especially classic titles that are in the public domain and required reading titles. It was December 2009, and every news story was about electronic reading devices. The Barnes and Noble Nook was delaying its release until January. The Sony e-book reader was allowing users to borrow e-book titles from libraries. The iPad was yet to be released. When we showed our student workers our new devices, they were baffled by the fact that they were not touch screen, backlit, or color. The Kindle DX was twice as expensive as the other devices. Had we made a mistake?

We learned a lot since that first floundering week with our Kindles. This is what we decided to do:

- Set up an Amazon account for Kindles (we called ours "PRHS Library").
- Purchase a gift card specifically for Kindle titles.
- Attach the gift card(s) to that account.
- Register each Kindle as Lib01-Lib20 through that single Amazon account.
- When the Kindle is registered, any user can use the wireless access, as long as they are within range of the Whispernet (Sprint's proprietary wireless 3G network used by Amazon to deliver titles and updates to the Kindle).
- Add titles from either the Amazon account or from the device itself. Titles within the public domain are free, although some cost a small amount and have additional formatting or features which can help the reader to navigate through the book. The titles are loaded wirelessly to each device.
- Each new title comes with six copies. When you purchase a new release, you get six copies to download. This helps extend your e-book purchasing budget if you have multiple devices.

We next decided to catalog each Kindle. We made the decision to make all 20 Kindles identical. Every time we download a book on one device, we download that title on all 20 devices (which means we purchase another three copies of it). So we created one single MARC record and attached 20 item records. We set the Kindles up as a different material type because we want them to circulate as a book (we circulate books for three weeks), but we want them counted as equipment (we track serial numbers and equipment inventory through our database, too).

If we were going to make the 20 Kindles different—that is, if we were going to have different titles on different Kindles—we would have created individual bibliographic records for each device and included a list of titles in the contents field for each Kindle. One idea that we had was to create themed Kindles. We imagined that a student would borrow the vampire Kindle and all of the titles on that Kindle would be vampire-themed. It seemed like a fun idea, but too difficult for us to manage.

We created some simple laminated cards to place in each Kindle case. The cards show the user several tips and tricks for navigating through the titles and the additional features.

We attended a meeting of the Special Education case workers and brought a Kindle for each of them. We showed them how their students could use the devices for changing font size, looking up words in the dictionary and encyclopedia, as well as turning on text-to-speech. The Special Education staff members were thrilled with the devices and planned to use them with reluctant readers to try to encourage some additional interest in reading.

We also attended a school board meeting and brought a Kindle for each member of the board. We showed them the power of the electronic book reader, demonstrating all of the features and thrilling them with our new technology.

I began adding titles that are the most read and most requested as well as new releases to each Kindle. As we circulated the devices to our faculty, we encouraged them to add titles that they wanted to read. I continually monitored our Amazon account, and teachers were not purchasing new titles. I'm not sure if they were hesitant to purchase titles on their own, or if they were truly pleased with the titles that I had preselected for each Kindle. Either way, I needed to add more titles so that we had a wider range of titles on each device.

My next test was with our school's book club. We have a mix of about ten high school students who meet monthly to read and discuss books with me. I decided to have them read our January title on the Kindle, rather than sharing print copies. I also encouraged each student to purchase any titles that they wanted using our library account. The students were stunned. They asked, "Shouldn't we have a limit?" and "Do you mean books that the teachers want us to read?" I told them no, explaining that I really wanted the Kindles filled with titles that students want to read, not what I think that they want to read—or worse, what they think that I think that they want to read. I wanted them to honestly purchase any titles that they want to read. I trusted our students with the device and with the decision to choose titles.

I monitored them daily through my Kindle Amazon account. I watched as they began by adding titles like *Animal Farm*, *The Scarlet Letter*, and *Wuthering Heights* (they are book club members after all). One student bought a Sudoku puzzle book, which, I am delighted to say, actually works. Another started purchasing the complete *Gossip Girls* collection, while still another bought a cookbook, a graphic novel, and several new releases. As we met to discuss our January book (Figure 6.3), we found ourselves mostly talking about the Kindles themselves. One student was concerned that her circulation statistics were falling drastically for the month. She had been on our "top 10 list" of students who checked out the most titles the month before. She said that she read at least 17 books on her Kindle in the four weeks that she had it.

Some students returned their device with little said. Others wanted to keep it longer. Still others said they loved reading books on it. One student said that she prefers print books but found it powerful to see a book described in a magazine and have

Figure 6.3. Students with Kindles

the ability to immediately purchase it and begin reading it within the minute. They all agreed that they read through some books that they would not necessarily have read before because "they were there." This is what I was hoping for. I love nothing more than serendipitous reading and learning!

Our principal has asked if we could trial some textbooks on the Kindles. I think textbooks on a Kindle is a powerful idea. However, none of our current textbook titles were available on the Kindle as of late winter 2010. He also suggested that the next step for our school would be to buy a Kindle for every freshmen and load it with textbooks, required reading, and recommended free-reading titles. It would certainly lighten a student's backpack, but would the cost eventually offset? If a student loses his copy of *Romeo and Juliet* today, he pays $5.00 to replace the paperback. If a student loses his copy of *Romeo and Juliet* on the Kindle, he owes us $400 for the cost of the device. (The titles are not actually lost as they can be moved from the lost device and replaced on a new device via our online account.)

Problems with Kindles

- Students expect touch screen, and so far, the Kindle is not available as a touch screen.
- The multidirectional button on the Kindle DX is clunky and lacks refinement, especially compared to the navigation on a device like the Sony Reader or the new iPad.
- They are expensive! (We had a student place her Kindle in her backpack within its padded case, and the pressure of her books cracked the screen. Through our extended warranty, our Kindle was replaced at no cost, but we get only one free replacement for each device.)

- While reading nonfiction especially, I find myself flipping back and forth through a book. I found this very difficult and nonintuitive with the Kindle.
- The OS is proprietary, so you are unable to borrow books from other e-reader services and you are unable to use the Kindle on a wireless network other than their Sprint network. (I do not receive their wireless at my house, so I was unable to shop at the store or use the lookup features from my home.)
- Some titles are not available in Kindle format. The state of New Hampshire's Big Read this spring was *To Kill a Mockingbird*, and it is unavailable on the Kindle. Frustrating!
- The Kindle does not display in color. Even if our science textbooks were available in Kindle format, it does not seem likely that the graphs and maps would be 100 percent useful in black and white.

I would say that the final negative is a feeling I get whenever I purchase new technology. What will the next version hold? As soon as we bought our Kindles, we worried that they seemed out of date. Should we have waited and purchased iPads or another multifunctional device? Will the next Kindle have a touch screen? Will it display in color?

My advice to anyone thinking of purchasing an e-reader is to try out a couple of different devices. If I had it to do all over again, I would not change a thing. After experimenting with several different e-readers, I still prefer the Kindle technology for a school environment. I love that our collections are truly student-centered. I also appreciate the robust collections available for the Kindle. The book is not dead, but long live the Kindle!

Social Networking

We also moved forward with the idea that we are guides into this world of social networking, open access, rather than gatekeepers. We began several years ago by diving in and creating a strong personal and professional social networking presence. Every step of the way, I thought of myself as a social networking guide.

In addition to creating a personal presence, the library squad created a PRHS Library presence. We set up a blog, a micro-blogging account, social networking fan sites, and a photo-sharing account. We created a consistent and lighthearted voice in all of our user-centered resources. We wanted users to actually read our blog and visit our fan sites. Some tools, like our photo-sharing account, are used simply to store resources to which we want online access. In addition, we turned on the OPAC's ability for students to rate and review library materials and showed all of our incoming students how to use it.

It is easy to feel like your library is a set of resources that needs to be protected from some malicious user. It's easy to think that you have to set up additional rules about protecting what you perceive to be your materials from these robbing no-goodniks. But libraries all over the world need to have this internal conversation. Trust your users, and they will learn to trust you.

Your To-Do List

✓ Put supplies and tools where your users can access them.

✓ Expand your library policies to show that you trust your users.

✓ Allow users to post comments, and to share information on your blogs and wikis

✓ Lobby for user access to wireless Internet in the library, e-mail for students, availability of social networking (especially micro-blogging, blogging, video sharing, bookmark sharing, and photo-sharing sites)

✓ Trust your users, and they will learn to trust you.

✓ Ask your students for input on big decisions regarding information access and new technologies.

✓ Trust your colleagues on social networking sites and be sure to always serve as an example of how to use these tools professionally.

✓ ($) Trust your users with developing a learner-centered collection on a device such as a Kindle.

7

Step Seven: Publicize

Take every opportunity that you can to share your successes with your users as well as your financial stakeholders (administration, school board, parents, and community). Once you receive funding and support from your community, it is crucial that you publicize everything that you have done. Write a newsletter and send it home to parents in the report card mailings. Create a monthly report including circulation statistics, class visits, and highlights to share with the administration and the school board. Write a book review blog or post a new picture of a happy user on your Web site once per week. Add information about your library into any school-wide publications. Send out entertaining e-mails announcing new video shipments to your faculty. Volunteer to speak in front of the faculty about a new database available via your Web site. There are many ways to publicize, and we need to do them all.

Personal interaction is one of the greatest promotions for your library that you can have. Through personal involvement in committees, contributions to building initiatives, and teaching alongside fellow faculty members, you are not only advertising your importance in the school community, but you are also demonstrating it. Make sure that your staff is greeting users, friendly and welcoming at Open Houses, and inviting to the rest of the community.

Create a quarterly newsletter, send it home to parents, and make it available to everybody via your Web site. Include library events like banned books week, teen read week, and national library month. Keep your community apprised about the great world of librarianship. But also keep most of the news local. Write brief articles about changes in your library, new staff members, new online databases, and projects that may be interesting. Include pictures of happy users utilizing your resources. Most importantly, create a section with measurements of library services. Include checkout statistics, gate counts, class visits, number of bibliographies created using your online citation tools, and statistics on searches in the online databases. We occasionally show historical statistics for a tool that has shown an increase as well as an explanation for the sudden boost in use. Keep the language conversational and easy to read. Think about who your audience is as you write each article. One of the most helpful things to do is to keep a list of topics for the newsletter and continue to add short articles between issues. This will help to keep the articles relevant and interesting instead of last-minute filler for the newsletter. Finally, be sure to locate and utilize a professional newsletter template (ours appears in Figure 7.1). Take some time before you send out your first issue to create an interesting format, and you can use the same template for years to come. A consistent and contemporary appearance will be recognizable, appropriate, and relevant well into the future.

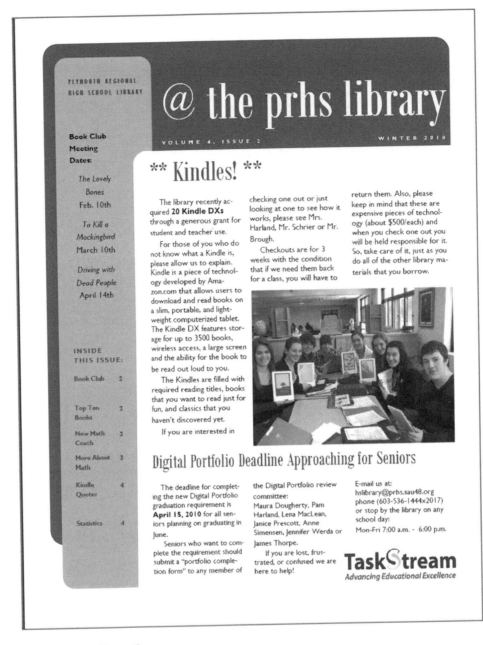

Figure 7.1.   Newsletter Front Cover

Create a monthly report (such as that shown in Figure 7.2) including circulation statistics, class visits, and library highlights to share with administration and the school board or trustees. Once again, take your time in establishing a template that shows your library is professional and relevant. Be sure to keep your design simple, like your Web site, with plenty of white space and color images of library users. The monthly report should indicate to your financial stakeholders exactly what goes on each month in your library. Show them the truth, and include information about levels of collaboration, historical statistics (so they have a constant place of comparison), and highlights that relate to them. Keep the administration informed about how your library shares resources, evaluates tools, and focuses on users.

February
2010

Plymouth Regional High School Library
Monthly Report

February 2010
Pam Harland, Librarian
Casey Brough, Assistant Librarian
Bob Schrier, Library Assistant
Lena MacLean, Digital Portfolio Instructor

Figure 7.2.   Library Report Front Cover

Keeping your community members informed about the services that your library offers is one of the most important things that you can do to keep a successful library thriving and supported. You will find support in all corners of the community when it comes to budgets, challenges, and scheduling. Readers will be more involved in decision making, funders will be more informed about how the money is being spent, and administrators will see the incredible impact that the library has on all aspects of the school. Feel free to brag, educate, and inform—just be sure to keep the tone professional and conversational, and the design neat and simple.

Providing a variety of ways for users to gather information about your library is crucial. In addition to the newsletter and library report, we also keep our users up to date with a blog. We have actually converted our blog into our library Web site (Figure 7.3). Provide links to your catalog of books, lists of online databases, local libraries and historical societies, research guides, digital portfolio information, library curriculum, and library mission and policies, as well as links to your newsletter and library report archives. In addition to all of the information that your users continually need, keep your blog current by adding an entry approximately once per week. Add book reviews, literary figure pieces, and current events. Like your newsletter and library reports, keep your Web design simple and easy to read with plenty of white space.

Your school or organization may already have several school-wide publications. Get short but pertinent articles into those publications as well. Advertise the library hours, special events, and the types of resources available from your library. Keep your information current and valuable. When you write a library newsletter and send it home to parents and out to the community, you can assume that not everybody will

Figure 7.3.   Library Web Site

read it. You can reach more people by including your library news in publications that a different audience does read.

You may also have a local or regional newspaper that publishes local-interest pieces. Call the local editors at least once each school year to include library events. Obviously, you will call when an author comes to your school or other large school-wide events. But you should also call the local paper occasionally to educate them about how access to information has changed and what you are doing to educate the community.

You are involved in several committees and organizations. Volunteer, when appropriate, to be the public spokesperson for your organization or committee. When your technology committee is asked to give a presentation to your school board about a change in policy, be the person to give the presentation. Keep your face and your name highly visible to the people who make decisions (both personnel and financial) in your school district. If you live in a large school district, you may find it difficult to get to know your school board. This creates an opportune time for them to connect a name with a face (assuming that they have been reading your newsletters and your monthly reports). If you live in a small community, you may know the members of your school board as neighbors, coaches, and even friends. Giving a presentation about technology or policy to the board is a perfect opportunity to display your professionalism. The more that people, like the school board and the administration, see you as a contributing member of the school community, the more they will respect you for your ideas and expertise.

The Plymouth Model

We began publicizing everything that was happening in the library by writing a library newsletter to be sent home to community members each quarter. We use a simple, clean, and professional-looking publishing software template to create the structure of the newsletter. We write about library events such as Banned Books Week, National Library Week, and Read Across America. We include biographies of our elite library squad, book reviews, book club news, and digital portfolio updates. Our most read section is our chart of statistics (Figure 7.4). We call it "Library By the Numbers" and try to include a wide variety of statistics. We change these statistics each quarter to keep the newsletter interesting.

We find it useful to keep a list of newsletter ideas so that when it comes time to actually write, it's not ideas that are lacking. Finally, we try each month to include something interesting for faculty members. We often include a new database feature, information on an interesting Web site, or specifics about a research project. Before the newsletter is mailed home, we print color copies out for our administration and school board and send a PDF to the faculty. We frequently discuss saving the paper and encouraging parents and community members to read the newsletter online, but whenever we publish a new issue, we get great feedback and are encouraged to continue printing it out. (See Appendix D for a sample newsletter.)

Monthly Reports

Where the newsletter has statistics on things such as "student who checked out the most books" and "number of bibliographies created during the month," we found that we wanted to share some more important data with the administration and school board. We started by submitting a monthly memo to the principal and superintendent including the number of books checked out with historical comparisons, so that they could see how money spent on materials was being heavily utilized by the students in our school.

We had been submitting an "end-of-year report" to our administration each year, which listed each class that came into the library for a scheduled lesson. I find it hard to believe that anybody from the administration did much more than skim through this 25-page list of classes and research topics. While it did provide them with a list that showed how very busy we were during the school year, there was nothing very relevant about it. We decided to take that year-end report and break it up into nine monthly reports.

Our monthly report is four pages long, and nearly half of it is filled up with pictures of happy students utilizing the library and its resources (Figure 7.5). We also include a bulleted list of "Highlights from the Month" including things like book displays, additions of resources, visits by other school districts, library celebrations,

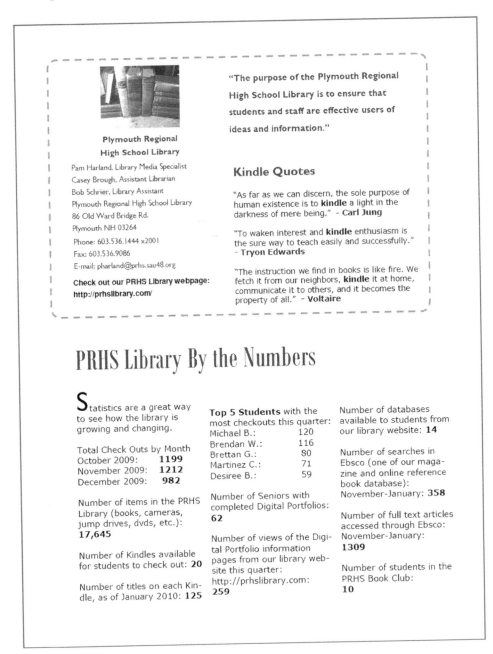

Figure 7.4.   Newsletter Statistics

tutoring highlights, digital portfolio statistics, and anything else that we want to tell the administration about.

In addition, we include monthly checkout statistics in comparison to some historical statistics. This is important, as we wanted to show the school board how much circulation has gone up since they increased our book budget during certain financial cycles.

Finally, we pick 10 class research projects to highlight. We describe the project, the grade level, and the faculty member who worked with us, and we include a level of collaboration. We use the level-of-collaboration rubric created by the Londonderry (NH) School District Librarians, but you could include any table or prose that shows

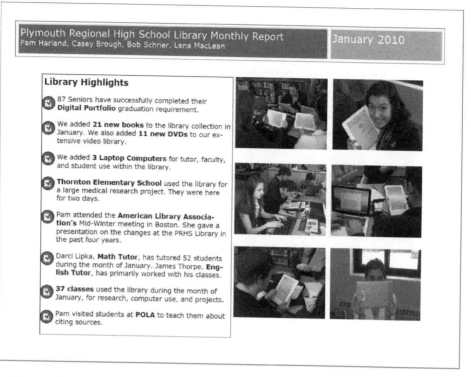

Figure 7.5.   Library Report Highlights Page

how closely you worked with the collaborating teacher on the project. Did you create the entire research projects? Are you giving book talks to five sections of freshmen in one day? Or did you simply reserve some computers so that a health class could word process for an hour?

At a local library conference, the school administrator of the year attended and spoke at one of our luncheons. He explained how valuable it was for him to have those kinds of statistics from his libraries. He told us that they could see that some libraries were presenting statistics of class use based on number of classes that walked through the door, but that was meaningless to him. He understood that having a class use the library to do word processing is drastically different from having a class use it to begin a research project that the faculty member and the librarian had created together. This inspired me to begin sharing the level of collaboration for each class that enters the library (Figure 7.6).

After I started presenting this data to our administration, one of the administrators asked me why I would include in my monthly report a class with which I did not fully collaborate. He thought that the report would have more of an impact if I included only 10 classes with which I fully collaborated. I explained that I share 10 classes each month because that gave me a good range to show the full spectrum of research and information-gathering projects that happen in the school every month. Choosing 10 is fun, because I could choose a variety of subjects, grades, and research topics to share. Also, I rarely have time to fully collaborate on 10 different research projects each month. I explained to the administrator that creating a research project with a faculty member is extremely time consuming, and that not all faculty members

| Plymouth Regional High School Library Monthly Report | | | | January 2010 |
| Pam Harland, Casey Brough, Bob Schrier, Lena MacLean | | | | |

Library Utilization and Collaboration Highlights: (not all classes using the library are listed)

Name or Topic of Unit (# of sections using the Library)	Grade Level and Subject Area	*Level of Collaboration				
		1	2	3	4	5
Poetry Out Loud research project	Ms. Boyd's Brit Lit classes		X			
The Spanish culture of bullfighting	Ms. Rella's Conversational Spanish Class		X			
Biographies of figures from American Literature	Ms. Dougherty's American Studies Classes					X
Geological systems research and computer use	Mr. McKenney's Geological Systems Class	X				
Citing Sources, using NoodleBib and EasyBib	Ms. Rich's POLA English Class				X	
Understanding loans: auto and student loans	Ms. Hughes' Pre-Calc Classes				X	
Great Depression research unit	Ms. Kimball's English 9 Classes					X
Recipe research	Ms. Paquette's Creative Cooking Class			X		
Journalism unit	Ms. Donahue's Creative Writing Class		X			
Middle Eastern geography and blog setup	Mr. Blais' Middle East Class			X		

*Level of Collaboration Rubric (developed by Londonderry High School LMC):

1. No collaboration beyond scheduling the library and offering assistance to teachers and students.	2. Pull together resources (online and print) for teachers and students to use in the library, curriculum lab, or classroom.	3. Provide instruction at the beginning of a unit as well as scheduling and pulling resources together.	4. Plan with teachers, offering suggestions and strategies as well as instruction, scheduling and pulling resources together.	5. Provide a lesson in an information literacy skill concept as a result of planning with teachers as well as scheduling and pulling resources together.

Figure 7.6.   Level of Collaboration Rubric

are looking for a collaborator. I continue to offer my assistance, but I realize that some faculty members have different priorities, and I will try to aid them in any way I can.

Be sure to set achievable goals with this effort. You do not want to promise to put together a monthly report, when in reality you only have time at the end of each quarter to complete it. I have found that at the beginning of the school year, I do not have time to create an August newsletter, so I begin the monthly reports with September and include any highlights that happened during the summer or during the first few days of August (if, in fact, school begins in August that year).

Online Publicity

Start a blog today. They are simple to set up and use. The most important thing that you can do before you start is have something to say. Make a decision to review new books that you acquire and post reviews on your blog. Make a decision that you are going to share your favorite technology tips via your new blog and make sure that you post a link, embed a video, or write your own tip each week. Make a decision that you are going to write a podcast blog where you post a new link to a podcast that has educational value for your faculty. Whatever it is that you are interested in and want to share with the world, be sure to set up a blog about it. You may find that you want to keep your blog strictly personal and fill it with your favorite recipes and photographs of your family. Or you may find that you want to have a blog specifically for a research project you are guiding students on. There are many ideas, and you may have two or three blogs in order to keep track of your entire digital professional and personal life.

Micro-blogging is a nice way to promote your library and its resources and services. We often post links to new book reviews, favorite relevant quotes or links to newsworthy articles. The most important use of micro-blogging for us has been when we post questions to our professional learning community. We often post questions about creating new policies, changing resources, or adding new technologies. We have found valuable responses by posting some very simple questions to our followers. Create multiple accounts, one personal, one for your library and you may post to both accounts from a micro-blogging tool. Ask people in your professional learning community what they use to monitor and post micro-blogs.

Establish a photo-sharing account so that you have an online receptacle for all of the photographs with which you populate your Web site, blogs, and newsletters. Including photographs in everything that you do is a great way to positively publicize your library. Remember that images of happy users in the context of your library is a fabulous publicity tool.

Your To-Do List

✓ Create a simple, easy-to-update, easy-to-read newsletter template and start writing!

✓ Brainstorm a list of resources, services, and tools you want to share with your community. Don't ever stop!

✓ Start a blog, and update it once per week with a conversational book review or reminder of an upcoming event.

✓ Start a micro-blogging account for you or your library and update it at least once per week with an idea, questions, or link.

✓ Read and reply to your e-mail.

✓ Volunteer to speak publicly, either in front of the faculty, the students, the school board, or other committee or group. Even if it isn't about the library, you are still spreading the word, more people are getting to know you, and you are visible.

✓ Make a contact at the local newspaper.

✓ Share a brief library-related resource or service story in a school-wide publication.

✓ Word of mouth publicity is the best publicity! Keep your users happy, and they will talk about their happy experiences.

Conclusion

Visualize this: you walk through your well-lit library space. Several students are gathered around a table creating a board game about Jungian psychology. Another group of students is sitting with the social studies tutor, debating what the political climate in New Hampshire would be like if the first presidential primary did not take place here. Back by the windows, a table of boys is taking notes into a digital voice recorder while they brainstorm a video that they will make for a Civil War project. Several individual students are sitting quietly within the book stacks reading a pile of poetry books that sit beside them. Two girls are giggling in the periodical section while reading an entertainment magazine. An English tutor is reviewing a senior's college essay. A table of students is doing their homework. A student is making photocopies of an assignment to hand out to her classmates for their reflection. Students are blogging, uploading files to their digital portfolios, uploading pictures from their mobile device to their network folders. Another student is helping herself to a jar of markers and a pair of scissors. You walk between the tables and students call you over to ask about citing sources on a board game, for a book recommendation to download to an e-book, and what the first election was in which you remember voting. Your library is thriving with inquiry, curious researchers, and sharing of information and resources. The shift has happened.

In order to keep your library relevant to the needs of your community, you need to make a change. The fundamental change is an attitudinal shift from being the protector and guardian of a legacy to being the guide to the exponential growth of the Internet and the resources that reside there. As you make this shift, there will be intimidating moments, but not making a change is even scarier. Not making the shift in your library service means decreasing funding for your space. Not making the shift in your library resources means decreasing users in your space. Not making the shift in your philosophy means decreasing significance in your community.

Challenges

In creating a more social environment for your users, you will find that noise levels increase. As students and faculty feel more ownership of the space, you will hear additional outbursts of laughter, passionate debates about topics, and other varieties of loud voices. We must constantly walk the fine line of how much noise is too much noise. Noise levels are one of the biggest challenges that we face. In order to lower the volume, be prepared to hand out headphones to your users. As everyone incorporates more audiovisual resources into projects, headphones will silence a lot of the background noise and isolate some of the students. Allowing your users to wear headphones may be a change in policy in your building, but it can greatly assist noise issues in a social space, and listening to music while working may help users to stay more focused on their own work. Since we provide audiobooks and encourage users to incorporate podcasts, music, and other audio files into projects, headphones were an easy policy change.

You may also find that faculty members who do not actually use the learning commons may assume that the library is now being used as a glorified, noisy study hall. Some departments may not support the new mission of the learning commons and refuse to send students or utilize services as their vision of a traditional library is not being met. Publicity will help to teach everyone what the goals in the new learning commons are.

As your learning commons becomes more heavily used, you may find it necessary to more actively monitor what students are doing on the computers. Are certain computer games allowed? If another student needs a computer for legitimate research and all of the computers are occupied, you may have to decide who is not using a computer for a legitimate academic purpose.

In order to remain current with new technologies, two things must take place: staff training, and a constant reinvestment in more modern technologies. Both of these items cost money and take time away for research and planning. Think about alternative methods of staff training and access to technology monies.

Many learning commons allow food and drink in order to create an even more social environment. This can generate a whole new set of issues within your library space. Local libraries that have changed their food-and-drink policy have surprisingly noticed that trash pickup is much easier. They noticed an immediate difference in users no longer hiding food packages and sneaking drink containers around the space. Our users often leave food wrappers and empty cups on top of the computers because it is a well-hidden space to hide their precious contraband. These are all issues that need to be considered and reevaluated every once in a while.

Like many people, you may be inclined to avoid risk-taking. The steps in this book describe a major shift in culture and service. This shift demands creative ways of thinking that may not come naturally to you. Perhaps you, like many librarians, gravitated toward librarianship because of the rules, customs, and structure in the traditional library model. It will require a shift in your professional goals because this is all about changing the rules, customs, and structure of the time-honored library model. Our users have outgrown that model. They now have another option for finding information. In the presence of more efficient, faster, and easier resources, the book room will vanish. With the information revolution, users have few reasons to patronize an old-fashioned library when looking for research. Shushing students, silent reading rooms, headphone bans, and cryptic language is out with the dusty and unread print reference books.

Final Thoughts

The basic philosophy of libraries remains unchanged. We continue to remain committed to supporting and promoting intellectual freedom, academic inquiry, and literacy of all kinds. We are just doing it with a different set of rules, policies, customs, patrons, and structure around us.

The first and most important priority is to be sure that your shift is user-centered rather than technology-centered, rule-centered, or resource-centered. Above all other things, your users need to be your libraries' main focus. Our focus should be on making locating information easier on them, and at the same time, it becomes easier on us. Once you trust and teach your users to be autonomous learners in your learning commons, they will teach themselves to locate the tools and resources that they need. We give them the basic experiential context in which to find certain information, and then they will extrapolate and apply that towards new and more complex information retrieval and use.

Next, be sure that your shift is made with flexibility and mobility in mind. You do not want to make a decision today that reflects some current fad or recent layout idea. Keep your redesigns, both physical and virtual, flexible. While libraries are often the space of permanence and a historic archive of materials, some aspects must be easily adaptable for the fast-paced changes in technology that we face on a daily basis. Let go of some control over your space and trust your users to customize the facility and resources themselves.

While looking at changes in your space, look to other departments with whom you can share resources. Also, publicize everything that you do. Keep your publicity positive, relevant, and lighthearted. You want your readers to actually enjoy reading about your learning commons.

Take any or all of these seven simple steps and you will move your library into the twenty-first century. Continue to ask yourself: in what world will our students be living and working, and what skills will they need to succeed? The next 5 and 10 years will hold more dramatic changes, and we must be prepared to adapt for our users. As information technologies change exponentially, how do you plan on remaining relevant for your users? If the last 10 years were any measure of what the future will hold, we can predict that it will be a wild ride.

If you cannot make this shift along with the shifts in information technologies, your users will leave you behind. Your specific decisions about implementation do not matter. It is imperative that you make a change and adapt for this new technology-driven world.

In a decade when libraries are losing funding, bookstores are being replaced by Internet giants, and print books are being discarded in favor of digital book readers, librarians need to make a decision. Are you going to go down with the ship, or will you find creative ways to survive? The choice is yours—but you have to act now!

Appendix A

PRHS Library Survey - for Students

1. PRHS Library Survey 2007

1. What grade are you in right now?

◯ Freshman (soon to be a Sophomore)

◯ Sophomore (soon to be a Junior)

◯ Junior (soon to be a Senior)

◯ Senior (just graduated!)

2. How often do you visit the library?

	Daily	Weekly	A Couple of Times per Month	Monthly	Occasionally	Never
Before school:	◯	◯	◯	◯	◯	◯
During school:	◯	◯	◯	◯	◯	◯
After school:	◯	◯	◯	◯	◯	◯

3. Why do you come to the library? (select all that apply)

☐ To do research for my classes

☐ To do homework/study

☐ To use the computers

☐ To check out library books

☐ To get book suggestions from Librarians

☐ To get help from the Librarians with Citing Sources

☐ To socialize

☐ To get help from the Librarians with Research

☐ To use the copy machine

Any other reason that we left off the list?

[   ]

4. How comfortable are you with asking for help in the library?

◯ Comfortable

◯ Hesitant

◯ Uncomfortable

Comments:

[   ]

5. The atmosphere in the PRHS Library is (select all that apply)

☐ Friendly   ☐ Academic   ☐ Alive

☐ Noisy   ☐ Busy   ☐ Helpful

☐ Quiet   ☐ Serious   ☐ Stupendous

☐ Comfortable   ☐ Strict   ☐ Confusing

☐ Welcoming   ☐ Calm

Other (please specify)

[   ]

2. PRHS Library Survey

1. Please rate the following resources & services:

	Very Valuable to me	Valuable to me	Somewhat Valuable to me	Not Valuable to me	I Didn't Know or Never Used
New Fiction Books	○	○	○	○	○
New Non-Fiction Books	○	○	○	○	○
Graphic Novels	○	○	○	○	○
Magazines & Newspapers	○	○	○	○	○
Reference Books (Dictionaries, atlases, etc.)	○	○	○	○	○
Audio Books	○	○	○	○	○
Noodle Tools	○	○	○	○	○
Wiki Research Pages	○	○	○	○	○
Online Databases (EBSCO, Newsbank, SIRS, etc.)	○	○	○	○	○
Helping You with Research & Projects	○	○	○	○	○
Able to Check Books Out Over the Summer	○	○	○	○	○
After School Hours Open Until 6 p.m.	○	○	○	○	○
Before School Hours Open by 7 a.m.	○	○	○	○	○

2. What do you like BEST about the library?

[   ]

3. What do you like LEAST about the library?

[   ]

4. Anything else that you would like us to know or suggestions you would like to make?

PRHS Library Survey - for Faculty

1. PRHS Library Survey 2007

1. Category (check one)

○ English   ○ Math   ○ Career/Technical
○ Fine Arts   ○ Computers   ○ Support Staff
○ Special Education ○ Social Studies   ○ Guidance & Health Services
○ Science   ○ Foreign Language ○ Administration

2. How often have you used the services of the PRHS Library this year?

☐ Daily   ☐ Several times a semester
☐ Several times a week   ☐ Rarely
☐ Once a week   ☐ Never

2. Rate the Following PRHS Library Resources and Services

3. Please rate the following resources:

	Very Valuable	Valuable	Somewhat Valuable	Not Valuable	Do Not Know/Never Used
Wiki Research Pages	○	○	○	○	○
Noodle Tools	○	○	○	○	○
New Fiction Books	○	○	○	○	○
New Non-Fiction Books	○	○	○	○	○
Graphic Novels	○	○	○	○	○
Audiobooks	○	○	○	○	○
Newsletter	○	○	○	○	○
New Videos/DVDs	○	○	○	○	○
Online Databases (Ebsco, Newsbank, etc.)	○	○	○	○	○

Comments:

4. Please rate the following services:

	Very Valuable	Valuable	Somewhat Valuable	Not Valuable	Do Not Know/Never Used
Books on Reserve for Research Projects	○	○	○	○	○
New Library Hours	○	○	○	○	○
Teaching Research Skills	○	○	○	○	○
Teaching Noodle Tools	○	○	○	○	○
Helping Students Find Books	○	○	○	○	○
Helping Students with Research & Projects	○	○	○	○	○
Helping You Find Materials & Information	○	○	○	○	○
Summer Reading and Check-Out	○	○	○	○	○
M&Ms	○	○	○	○	○

Comments:

5. What resources and/or services do you want to know more about?

6. Are there services not being offered by the PRHS Library that you would like to see?

7. The atmosphere in the PRHS Library is

☐ Friendly	☐ Academic	☐ Alive
☐ Noisy	☐ Busy	☐ Helpful
☐ Quiet	☐ Serious	☐ Wonderful
☐ Comfortable	☐ Strict	☐ Confusing
☐ Welcoming	☐ Calm	

Other (please specify)

1. Circulation of books and other library materials has dramatically increased this past year. Have you noticed your student bringing home and reading more books and library materials?

◯ Yes

◯ No

◯ Haven't noticed a change

Comments:

2. The PRHS Library is now open until 6 p.m. Monday through Friday. How often does your student utilize these new extended hours?

◯ Daily

◯ Weekly

◯ Occasionally

◯ Rarely

◯ Never

◯ Don't Know

Comments:

3. In your opinion, what is your student's attitude towards the PRHS Library's resources and services?

◯ Positive

◯ Negative

◯ Don't Know

Comments:

4. We have sent two issues of the PRHS Library Newsletter home with report cards this year. Did you find the information valuable?

◯ Yes

◯ No

◯ Did not read

Comments:

5. Would you like to continue receiving the PRHS Library Newsletter?

◯ Yes, continue to include with report cards

◯ Yes, send electronically (post on website or via email)

◯ Not interested

Comments:

6. If your student needs to do research for a school project, where does he or she typically go? (check all that apply)

☐ Internet access at home

☐ Public Library

☐ PRHS School Library

☐ Don't Know

☐ Other (please specify)

7. If you have any comments, opinions, or suggestions for the PRHS Library, please feel free to enter them here:

PRHS LIBRARY SCAVENGER HUNT

1. Go to the Library website: prhslibrary.com
   Click on Find A Book.

2. Search for a book on one of the following topics:
   Zombies
   Spiders
   Basketball

   Can you tell which books are available or not?

   Tell us how:

3. Choose one book from the results list and write the call number or letters in the label below.

4. Find the book on the shelf.
   (Ask for help if you can't find it!)
   Take your book to the check-out desk.

   The student worker will stamp your sheet here:

   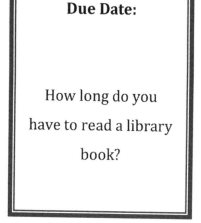

   Due Date:

   How long do you have to read a library book?

From *The Learning Commons: Seven Simple Steps to Transform Your Library* by Pamela Colburn Harland. Santa Barbara, CA: Libraries Unlimited. Copyright © 2011.

5. Ask the student worker where to return library books.
   Put your book in the book return slot before the due date!

6. Find a copy of a magazine that looks interesting to you.
   Photocopy the cover.
   Attach the copy to this packet.
   Put the magazine back in the proper slot.

7. Politely introduce yourself to a librarian.
   Ask a librarian what his or her favorite book is and write the answer below

   ```



   ```

8. Browse through the Fiction section and find a book that looks interesting to you.
   Write down the title of the book:

   ```



   ```

   Leave the book on the book shelving cart at the check-out desk.

9. What channel is the TV on?

10. List a **biography** title that each member of your group might be interested in reading next year:

11. Go to the Library website.
    What time does the library close during the school year?

12. What book is featured in the Big Read? (Hint: It's on the bulletin board and on the website)

13. Go to the Library website.
Find the World Geography page under Research Pages.
What is the World Population right now?

(Hint: use the world clock)

14. Name something that you see out the window of the Library:

15. Go back to the Library website.
Mouse over DATABASES in the menu bar. Click on EBSCO.
The username is: ******
The password is: *****
Select the Student Research Center
Search for "Waterville Valley"
Pick one of the newspaper or magazine article headlines by clicking on the blue link.
Print the article out by clicking on the "Print" icon at the top of the EBSCO page.
Choose the printer called Library Copier.
Staple the printout to this sheet.

16. Are there any games in the Library?
(hint: there is a drawer labeled "games" in the supply cabinets)
Name one!

From *The Learning Commons: Seven Simple Steps to Transform Your Library*
by Pamela Colburn Harland. Santa Barbara, CA: Libraries Unlimited. Copyright © 2011.

17. What book do you think is the biggest in the Library?

18. How many TVs are in the Library?
(hint: there are more than one)

19. Use a ruler to measure the pencil sharpener. How long is it?

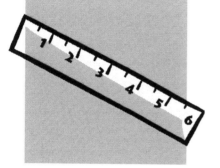

20. Draw a picture of you and your partner.
You can use the computer OR markers.
Ask Mr. Brough to hang it on his bulletin board.

21. How many computers are in the Library?

22. How many books do you think we have in the Library?

Appendix B

Plymouth Regional High School Library
Works Cited Format (MLA)
For a Research Paper

Listed below are examples of Works Cited formats for common types of materials.
If you need help with the citation for any source, see the Librarian.

BOOK WITH ONE AUTHOR
Author. *Title*. Place of Publication: Publisher, Date. Medium of publication consulted (*Print*).

Almond, Steve. *Candyfreak*. Chapel Hill: Algonquin Books, 2004. Print.

BOOK WITH NO AUTHOR'S NAME GIVEN
Title of Book. Place of Publication: Publisher, Date of Publication. Medium of publication

consulted (*Print*).

Sixteen Short Stories about Candy: An Anthology. New York: Dutton, 1985. Print.

WORK OR PIECE WITHIN AN ANTHOLOGY OR COLLECTION
Author of Work or Piece. "Work or Piece Title." *Title of Anthology*. editor or compiler of

Anthology. Place of Publication: Publisher, Date of Publication. page numbers. Medium

of publication consulted (*Print*).

Cheever, Mary. "The Need for Chocolate." *Candy Poems*. Ed. by Jerry White. New York:

Hyperion, 2005. 32-33. Print.

MLA Works Cited Direction update 9/09 PRHS Library

From *The Learning Commons: Seven Simple Steps to Transform Your Library*
by Pamela Colburn Harland. Santa Barbara, CA: Libraries Unlimited. Copyright © 2011.

MAGAZINE ARTICLE
Author of artice. "Article Title." *Magazine Title*. Date of Magazine: pages. Medium of

publication consulted (*Print*).

Moscowitz, Clara. "Getting Drunk on Chocolate in 1100 B.C." *Discover Magazine*. 7 Apr. 2008:

37-38. Print.

or via the Internet (include date of access; URL is optional)

Moscowitz, Clara. "Getting Drunk on Chocolate in 1100 B.C." *Discover Magazine*. 7 Apr. 2008.

Web. 30 August 2009. <http://discovermagazine.com/2008/apr/getting>.

INTERVIEW
Name of Person interviewed. Interview format. Date of Interview.

Parsons, Bruce. Personal interview. 8 Sep. 2009.

DVD (film or video recording)
Title. Director. Based on a novel or story by Author. Performers. Production Company, Date of

Release. Medium of publication consulted (*DVD*).

Charlie and the Chocolate Factory. Dir. Tim Burton. Based on a novel by Roald Dahl. Perf.

Johnny Depp and Helena Bonham Carter. Warner Brothers, 2005. DVD.

ONLINE MEDIA (film or video recording)
Author's Name (if available). "Title of File, Document, or Video." Date or Date of Last Revision.

    Title of Website on which clip is located. Medium of publication (*Web*). Access date.

    <URL: optional>.

Helge, Jan. "Baking: How to Make Chocolate Cake." 2 June 2007. *YouTube.* Web. 30 August

    2009. <http://www.youtube.com/v/au_c7aXeMOg&hl=en&fs=1>.

LECTURE (lecture, speech, address, or reading)
Name of Speaker. "Title of Lecture." Sponsoring Organization, Location. Date. Descriptive label

    (*Lecture, Speech, Address, Reading*).

Paquette, Madelyn. "Cooking with Chocolate." PRHS. Plymouth, NH. 15 Oct. 2009. Lecture.

ARTWORK
Name of artist. *Title of Artwork.* Medium of Artwork. Date artwork created. Museum, gallery, or

    collection where artwork is housed or source in which artwork is published, City where

    museum, gallery, or collection is located.

Klimt, G. *The Kiss.* Oil on Canvas. 1907. Oesterreichische Galerie im Belvedere, Vienna.

or accessed via the Internet

Klimt, G. *The Kiss* (1907). Oesterreichische Galerie im Belvedere, Vienna. *Art Collectors'*

    Guild. Web. Retrieved September 12, 2009, from <http://www.artcollectorsguild.com>.

MLA Works Cited Direction update 9/09 PRHS Library

INTERNET

Author (if available). "Article Title." *Website*. Publisher or Sponsor of the site (or N.p.), Date on

Webpage (or n.d.). Medium of publication (*Web*). Date of Access <URL: optional>.

"History of Chocolate." *Chocolates*. Kara Chocolates. 2000. Web. 24 Oct. 2009

<http://www.karachocolates.com/chochist.html>.

PERIODICAL ARTICLE CONTAINED WITHIN AN ONLINE DATABASE

Author of Article. "Article Title." *Name of Periodical,* Date Article was Published: Pages. *Name*

of Database. Medium of publication (*Web*). Date accessed <URL: optional>.

Soref, Anna. "Sweet News About Chocolate." *Better Nutrition,* Oct. 2006: 60-62. *MAS Ultra -*

School Edition. Web. 12 Oct. 2009 <http://search.ebscohost.com/22434276 >.

BLOG (weblog)

Name of author. "Title of blog entry." *Name of blog*. Date of blog entry. Medium of publication

(*Web*). Date of access. <Blog URL: optional>.

Lockett, Kath. "Mint-tastic M&Ms." *Chocablog*. 15 Aug. 2009. Web. 29 Aug. 2009.

<http://www.chocablog.com/>.

Works Cited

Almond, Steve. *Candyfreak*. Chapel Hill: Algonquin Books, 2004. Print. [book]

Charlie and the Chocolate Factory. Dir. Tim Burton. Based on a novel by Roald Dahl. Perf.

Johnny Depp and Helena Bonham Carter. 2005. Warner Bros. DVD. [DVD]

Cheever, Mary. "The Need for Chocolate." *Candy Poems*. Ed. Jerry White. New York: [Story within an anthology]

Hyperion, 2005. 32-33. Print. [YouTube Video]

Helge, Jan. *Baking: How to Make a Chocolate Cake*. *YouTube*. 2 June 2007. Web. 30 Aug. 2009.

<http://www.youtube.com/v/au_c7aXeMOg&hl=en&fs=1>.

"History of Chocolate." *Chocolates*. Kara Chocolates, 2000. Web. 24 Oct. 2006. [website]

<http://www.karachocolates.com/chochist.html>.

Klimt, G. *The Kiss*. 1907. Oesterreichische Galerie im Belvedere, Vienna. *Art Collectors' Guild*. [work of art on a website]

Web. 12 Sept. 2007. <http://www.artcollectorsguild.com/detail>.

- - -. *The Kiss*. 1907. Oil on Canvas. Oesterreichische Galerie im Belvedere, Vienna. [Same work of art]

Lockett, Kath. "Mint-tastic M&Ms." *Chocablog*. N.p., n.d. Web. 29 Aug. 2008. [blog]

<http://www.chocablog.com>.

McMurray, Shandley. "Foods that Soothe." *Chatelaine* Oct. 2006: 156-158. *MAS Ultra - School*

Edition. Web. 12 Oct. 2006. <http://search.ebscohost.com/ [Subscription database: EBSCO]

login.aspx?direct=true&db=ulh&AN=22271294&site=src-live>.

Moscowitz, Clara. "Getting Drunk on Chocolate in 1100 B.C." *Discover* 7 Apr. 2008: 37-38.

Print. [magazine article]

- - -. "Getting Drunk on Chocolate in 1100 B.C." *Discover* 7 Apr. 2008: n. pag. Web. 30 Aug.

2009. <http://discovermagazine.com/2008/apr/getting>. [Same magazine article on the Internet]

Paquette, Madelyn. "Cooking with Chocolate." PRHS. Plymouth, NH. 15 Oct. 2009. Lecture.

[Class lecture]

Parsons, Bruce. Personal interview. 8 Sept. 2009. [interview]

Sixteen Short Stories about Chocolate: An Anthology. New York: Dutton, 1985. Print.

[anthology]

Plymouth Regional High School Library
In-Text Citations (MLA)

If you need help with the in-text citation for any source, see a Librarian.

The MLA guidelines require that you cite quotations, summaries, paraphrases, and other material used from sources within parentheses placed at the end of the sentence in which the quoted or paraphrased material appears. These in-text parenthetical citations correspond to the Works Cited page found at the end of your paper. On-line sources follow the same pattern as print versions.

Type of Entry	Works Cited Entry (generated using NoodleBib)	In-Text Citation
book with single author	Almond, Steve. *Candyfreak.* Chapel Hill: Algonquin Books, 2004. Print.	(Almond 23)
website	*Kara Chocolates.* Web. 24 Oct. 2006 http://www.karachococolates.com>.	(Kara Chocolates) *or mention in your text "According to the Kara Chocolates website…"*
story or poem within an anthology or collection	Cheever, Mary. "The Need for Chocolate." *Candy Poems.* Ed. Jerry White. New York: Hyperion, 2005. 32-33. Print.	(Cheever 32)
YouTube video (or other online media)	Helge, Jan. *Baking: How to Make a Chocolate Cake.* 2 June 2007. *YouTube.* Web. 30 Aug. 2008 <http://www.youtube.com/v/au_c7aXeMOg&hl=en&fs=1>.	(Helge) *or mention in your text: "Helge's video analysis demonstrates…"*

To create your Works Cited list, sign up for a NoodleBib account.

Appendix C

PRHS Digital Portfolio Rubric for the Class of 2010

Portfolio Expectation	Distinguished	Proficient	Unsatisfactory
Acquire Information	__ No spelling or grammar errors. __ **3** or more samples of work. __ Reflection for each work sample. __ Reflections include what the artifact is, what was learned, and how work demonstrates proficiency. __ Best work identified and completion statement included. Met expectation ☐	__ A few spelling or grammar errors. __ **2** or more samples of work. __ Reflection for some work samples. __ Reflections include 2 out of 3 questions answered. __ Best work identified but completion statement is incomplete. Met expectation ☐	__ Several spelling or grammar errors. __ Insufficient number of work samples. __ Insufficient number of reflections. __ Insufficient quality of reflections. __ No best work identified. ☐
Think Critically	__ No spelling or grammar errors. __ **3** or more samples of work. __ Reflection for each work sample. __ Reflections include what the artifact is, what was learned, and how work demonstrates proficiency. __ Best work identified and completion statement included. Met expectation ☐	__ A few spelling or grammar errors. __ **2** or more samples of work. __ Reflection for some work samples. __ Reflections include 2 out of 3 questions answered. __ Best work identified but completion statement is incomplete. Met expectation ☐	__ Several spelling or grammar errors. __ Insufficient number of work samples. __ Insufficient number of reflections. __ Insufficient quality of reflections. __ No best work identified. ☐
Communicate Effectively	__ No spelling or grammar errors. __ **3** or more samples of work. __ Reflection for each work sample. __ Reflections include what the artifact is, what was learned, and how work demonstrates proficiency. __ Best work identified and completion statement included. Met expectation ☐	__ A few spelling or grammar errors. __ **2** or more samples of work. __ Reflection for some work samples. __ Reflections include 2 out of 3 questions answered. __ Best work identified but completion statement is incomplete. Met expectation ☐	__ Several spelling or grammar errors. __ Insufficient number of work samples. __ Insufficient number of reflections. __ Insufficient quality of reflections. __ No best work identified. ☐
Perform Civic Duties / Demonstrate Digital Citizenship	__ No spelling or grammar errors. __ **3** or more samples of work. __ Reflection for each work sample. __ Reflections include what the artifact is, what was learned, and how work demonstrates proficiency. __ Best work identified and completion statement included. Met expectation ☐	__ A few spelling or grammar errors. __ **2** or more samples of work. __ Reflection for some work samples. __ Reflections include 2 out of 3 questions answered. __ Best work identified but completion statement is incomplete. Met expectation ☐	__ Several spelling or grammar errors. __ Insufficient number of work samples. __ Insufficient number of reflections. __ Insufficient quality of reflections. __ No best work identified. ☐

Student Name: _____ Year of Graduation: **2010**

Portfolio Expectation	Distinguished	Proficient	Unsatisfactory
Provide Positive Student Profile	__ No spelling or grammar errors. __ Appropriate original or cited image(s) included. __ Statement is positive and detailed. __ Page layout is creative and well-organized. Met expectation: ☐	__ A few spelling or grammar errors. __ Appropriate original or cited image(s) included. __ Statement is positive but lacks detail. __ Page layout is well-organized. Met expectation: ☐	__ Several spelling or grammar errors. __ Image and/or statement missing or inappropriate. __ Image is not original or not cited. __ No attention to page layout. ☐
Include Innovative Software / Tools The list is not limited to the samples below.	__ Work samples are created using 5 or more different types of software or tools. (See checklist below.) Met expectation: ☐	__ Work samples are created using 3 or more different types of software or tools. (See checklist below.) Met expectation: ☐	__ Work samples are created using 2 or less different types of software or tools. (See checklist below.) ☐

Samples of Innovative Software & Tools Checklist:

__ Word Document
__ Excel Spreadsheet
__ Power Point Presentation
__ GIF or JPG Image (original or cited)
__ Video
__ Music Recording
__ Sound Recording/Podcast

__ Website
__ Publisher Presentation (brochure, sign)
__ Social Networking
__ PDF File (graphs, brochures, transcripts)
__ Electronic Booklet (PDF)
__ Hyperlinks
__ Blog/Wiki
__ Other

Digital Portfolios must show proficiency in each expectation.

Digital Portfolio Performance: Pass- Fail Date Submitted: Reviewed By:	

Appendix D

@ the prhs library

VOLUME 4, ISSUE 2   WINTER 2010

** Kindles! **

The library recently acquired **20 Kindle DXs** through a generous grant for student and teacher use.

For those of you who do not know what a Kindle is, please allow us to explain. Kindle is a piece of technology developed by Amazon.com that allows users to download and read books on a slim, portable, and lightweight computerized tablet. The Kindle DX features storage for up to 3500 books, wireless access, a large screen and the ability for the book to be read out loud to you.

The Kindles are filled with required reading titles, books that you want to read just for fun, and classics that you haven't discovered yet.

If you are interested in checking one out or just looking at one to see how it works, please see Mrs. Harland, Mr. Schrier or Mr. Brough.

Checkouts are for 3 weeks with the condition that if we need them back for a class, you will have to return them. Also, please keep in mind that these are expensive pieces of technology (about $500/each) and when you check one out you will be held responsible for it. So, take care of it, just as you do all of the other library materials that you borrow.

Digital Portfolio Deadline Approaching for Seniors

The deadline for completing the new Digital Portfolio graduation requirement is **April 15, 2010** for all seniors planning on graduating in June.

Seniors who want to complete the requirement should submit a "portfolio completion form" to any member of the Digital Portfolio review committee: Maura Dougherty, Pam Harland, Lena MacLean, Janice Prescott, Anne Simensen, Jennifer Werda or James Thorpe.

If you are lost, frustrated, or confused we are here to help!

E-mail us at: hslibrary@prhs.sau48.org phone (603-536-1444x2017) or stop by the library on any school day:
Mon-Fri 7:00 a.m. - 6:00 p.m.

Advancing Educational Excellence

Featured Non-Fiction

Beowulf on the Beach : What to Love and What to Skip in Literature's 50 Greatest Hits by Jack Murnighan

Do you feel guilty for not reading or not enjoying the so-called "great books"? Don't worry about it, it's not really your fault. Did anyone tell you that *Anna Karenina* is a beach read, that Dickens is hilarious, and that the *Iliad*'s battle scenes rival Hollywood's for gore?

Beowulf on the Beach is a funny field guide for helping you to read and really enjoy the books that you are often assigned in classes. Books you may think of as boring will take on new meaning after reading this hilarious guide.

Call #: 809 MUR

Winter Book Club Titles

Graceling
by Kristin Cashore

The Lovely Bones
by Alice Sebold

To Kill a Mockingbird by
Harper Lee

In March 2010 we invite you to be a part of The Big Read : New Hampshire Reads *To Kill a Mockingbird*. Public libraries, schools, and bookstores throughout the state will be hosting book discussions related to Harper Lee's novel.

The PRHS Book Club will be meeting on March 10th at 2:30 in the Library for our discussion. Please join us! Contact Mrs. Harland for more info: pharland@prhs.sau48.org.

A Decade of Books

I was just looking at the library book database and noticed that we have been checking out books via our online system for over 10 years now. Check out this list of the top ten titles over the last decade:

Title	Author	Number of Checkouts
Crank	Ellen Hopkins	202
Twilight	Stephenie Meyer	169
New Moon	Stephenie Meyer	128
Eclipse	Stephenie Meyer	109
Nineteen Minutes	Jodi Picoult	96
Burned	Ellen Hopkins	86
Just Listen	Sarah Dessen	75
City of Bones	Cassandra Clare	74
Acceleration	Graham McNamee	73
Glass	Ellen Hopkins	68

To see the other titles available from our library go to: http://prhslibrary.com and select "Find A Book" from the menu.

@ THE PRHS LIBRARY

Tutor Profile: Introducing Ms. Darci Lipka

Hi, everyone. My name is Darci Lipka and I'm the Mathematics Coach here at Plymouth Regional High School. Some of you may recognize me from last year when I was a Special Education Aide. I am very excited to have the opportunity to be a Math Coach this year and I've already been able to work with a number of wonderful students.

Math has always been a strong subject for me. I earned my Bachelor's degree in Accounting in 2001 from Suffolk University in Boston. I worked in the corporate world of Boston for about six years after graduation and never found it very fulfilling. I decided to pursue educa-

tion in the summer of 2007 and haven't missed the corporate world since! I moved to the Plymouth area about a year and a half ago and was lucky enough to land a job at PRHS. I'm also pursuing my Master's of Education in Math Education at Plymouth State University.

So what does a Math Coach do, you ask? Well, so far I've helped kids with their homework problems and helped them prepare for tests and quizzes. I've also done some work in small groups, brushing up on material from previous math courses. We can spend an entire block together or just 5 minutes to clarify a method or problem.

On regular school days I'm avail-

able in the PRHS library 2nd, 3rd and 4th block of the day. In addition to tutoring in the library, I teach Geometry at Pemi-Baker Academy during the 1st block of the day, and back at PRHS I teach Freshmen Seminar and Sophomore Enrichment classes.

I look forward to helping students at all levels of math for the rest of the school year. Bring your math binder and your thinking cap and we'll figure this math stuff out together!

More About Math

The PRHS Library has more to offer math students. We have textbooks in case you forgot your book while getting work done in the library. PRHS students in Algebra 1 and Algebra 2: Remember that your textbook is available online at www.pearsonsuccessnet.com.

Ask your math teacher for your access code today and stop carrying that heavy book around!

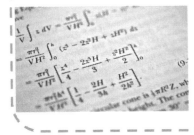

The library also has calculators, protractors, rulers, and compasses for you to use as well as an assortment of math software on our computers.

In addition to Ms. Lipka we also have Mr. Fogarty in the library to help students during Sophomore Structured Study.

Online Math Resources
www.purplemath.com From Algebra to Trigonometry, this site offers step by step, easy to follow tutorials.

www.cut-the-knot.org This site provides interactive ways to learn Algebra, Geometry and Calculus and also offers math games, puzzles and logic.

www.algebra.com Here you can get help with your Pre-Algebra, Algebra 1, Algebra 2 and Geometry homework. There are lessons, practice problems and quizzes on a multitude of topics.

www.mathforum.org Hosted by Drexel University, this site allows you to ask Dr. Math questions. You can also search for old questions that have already been answered by Dr. Math if you need help instantly.

www.mathworld.wolfram.com This site offers step by step tutorials on Algebra, Geometry, Calculus, Number Theory, Probability and Statistics

**Plymouth Regional
High School Library**

Pam Harland, Library Media Specialist

Casey Brough, Assistant Librarian

Bob Schrier, Library Assistant

Plymouth Regional High School Library

86 Old Ward Bridge Rd.

Plymouth NH 03264

Phone: 603.536.1444 x2001

Fax: 603.536.9086

E-mail: pharland@prhs.sau48.org

Check out our PRHS Library webpage:
http://prhslibrary.com/

"The purpose of the Plymouth Regional High School Library is to ensure that students and staff are effective users of ideas and information."

Kindle Quotes

"As far as we can discern, the sole purpose of human existence is to **kindle** a light in the darkness of mere being." - **Carl Jung**

"To waken interest and **kindle** enthusiasm is the sure way to teach easily and successfully." - **Tryon Edwards**

"The instruction we find in books is like fire. We fetch it from our neighbors, **kindle** it at home, communicate it to others, and it becomes the property of all." - **Voltaire**

PRHS Library By the Numbers

Statistics are a great way to see how the library is growing and changing.

Total Check Outs by Month
October 2009:   **1199**
November 2009:   **1212**
December 2009:   **982**

Number of items in the PRHS Library (books, cameras, jump drives, dvds, etc.): **17,645**

Number of Kindles available for students to check out: **20**

Number of titles on each Kindle, as of January 2010: **125**

Top 5 Students with the most checkouts this quarter:
Michael B.:   120
Brendan W.:   116
Brettan G.:   80
Martinez C.:   71
Desiree B.:   59

Number of Seniors with completed Digital Portfolios: **62**

Number of views of the Digital Portfolio information pages from our library website this quarter: http://prhslibrary.com: **259**

Number of databases available to students from our library website: **14**

Number of searches in Ebsco (one of our magazine and online reference book database): November-January: **358**

Number of full text articles accessed through Ebsco: November-January: **1309**

Number of students in the PRHS Book Club: **10**

Index

About the Author

PAMELA COLBURN HARLAND is a librarian, a real library zealot. She currently serves as the librarian at Plymouth Regional High School in Plymouth, New Hampshire. She has worked as a librarian in other school libraries, public libraries, university libraries, and at the Federal Reserve Bank of Boston's Research Library.

Pam holds the Intellectual Freedom chair on the New Hampshire School Library Media Association and especially enjoys fighting for the right for students in New Hampshire to have access to all kinds of information. Pam received the Intellectual Freedom Award in 2009, and she is the recipient of the 2010 New Hampshire Excellence in Education Award for Educational Media Professionals.

She lives in Rumney, New Hampshire, with her husband Russ and her two dogs Mr. Sparkle and Steve McQueen.

49507186R00075

Made in the USA
Lexington, KY
09 February 2016